WILLIAM SHAKESPEARE

HAMLET

CLASSICS

Published 2024

FiNGERPRINT! CLASSICS
Prakash Books

 Fingerprint Publishing
 @FingerprintP
 @fingerprintpublishingbooks
www.fingerprintpublishing.com

ISBN: 978 93 8777 934 1

William Shakespeare began his career as an actor, writer, and part owner of a playing company called the Lord Chamberlain's Men, later known as King's Men, in London. Often regarded as the 'Bard of Avon' he is one of the world's pre-eminent dramatists. Born and brought up in Stratford-upon-Avon, he married Anne Hathaway at the age of eighteen and they had three children—Susanna, and twins Hamnet and Judith. Though few records survive of his private life, he appeared to have retired to Stratford around 1613 where he died three years later.

His works still in existence, including some collaborations, consist of thirty-eight plays, one hundred and fifty-four sonnets, two long narrative poems, and several other verses. His plays are performed much more than any other playwright's and have been translated in almost all major languages. Most of his known works have been produced between 1589 and 1613. His early plays were mainly comedies and histories which remain regarded as some of the best works produced in these genres.

Shakespeare's plays are difficult to date. His early classical and Italianate comedies contain tight double plots and precise comic sequences giving way to the romantic atmosphere of his most acclaimed comedies in the mid-1590s. *A Midsummer Night's Dream*—a witty mixture of romance, fairy magic, and comic low life scenes—is one of his most delightful creations shortly before he turned to *Romeo and Juliet*. *Romeo and Juliet* is his most famous romantic tragedy of sexually charged adolescence, love, and death. It marks a departure from his earlier works and from others of the English Renaissance.

His plays demonstrate the expansiveness of his imagination and the extent of his learning. Shakespeare's sequence of great comedies continues with *Merchant of Venice*, *Much Ado About Nothing*, *As You Like It*, and *Twelfth Night*. He introduced prose comedy in the histories of the late 1590s—*Henry IV, Part I* and *Henry IV, Part II*, and *Henry V*—after the lyrical *Richard II*. *Julius Caesar* introduced a new kind of drama.

Shakespeare wrote the so-called 'problem plays' in the early 17th century. *Measure for Measure*, *Troilus and Cressida*, and *All's Well that Ends Well* being a few of them. Until about 1608, he mainly wrote tragedies including *Hamlet*, *Othello*, *King Lear*, and *Macbeth*. *Antony and Cleopatra* and *Coriolanus*—his last major tragedies, contain some of his finest poetry. Shakespeare wrote tragicomedies, also known as romances, in his last phase. These include *Cymbeline*, *The Winter's Tale*, and *The Tempest*, as well as the collaboration *Pericles, Prince of Tyre*.

A true genius, Shakespeare's popular characters and plots are studied, performed, reinterpreted, and discussed till today. William Shakespeare, known as the English national poet, is considered the greatest dramatist of all time.

CONTEXT

The earliest of the great tragedies, *Hamlet* was written in the early seventeenth century. It was entered in the Register of the Stationers' Company in July 1602 and was first published in printed form in 1603 followed by an enlarged edition in 1604. Always writing for the contemporary theatre, Shakespeare manipulated the Elizabethan stage with great resources and invention. He derived his ideas and stories from earlier literary works, a common practise during the sixteenth and seventeenth centuries. The legend of Amleth, preserved in *Gesta Danorum* by a twelfth-century chronicler Saxo Grammaticus, and a prose work by the French writer François de Belleforest, entitled *Histoires Tragiques*, are the possible sources from where the story of *Hamlet* was derived.

A play in which verse is used with great skill, *Hamlet* is a story of murder, suicide, madness—to those who call for melodrama—but for others it is a most subtle analysis of character. The raw material that Shakespeare appropriated in writing this play is the story of a Danish prince whose uncle murders the King, marries the Queen, and claims the throne. The prince pretends to be feeble-minded to throw his uncle off guard and manages to take revenge by killing him. Shakespeare changed the emphasis of this story entirely. His primary purpose was to satisfy his audience, but this was not enough, for he had to satisfy himself. His Hamlet was a philosophically minded prince who delays action because his knowledge of his uncle's crime is uncertain. Shakespeare went far beyond making uncertainty a personal quirk of Hamlet's and introduced a number of important ambiguities into the play that even the audience cannot resolve with certainty. For instance, whether Hamlet's mother, Gertrude, shares in Claudius's guilt; whether Hamlet continues to love Ophelia even as he spurns her, in Act III; whether Ophelia's death is suicide or accident; whether the ghost offers reliable knowledge, or seeks to deceive and tempt Hamlet; and, perhaps most importantly, whether Hamlet would be morally justified in taking revenge on his uncle. Shakespeare makes it clear that the stakes riding on some of these questions are enormous—

the actions of these characters bring disaster upon an entire kingdom. At the play's end it is not even clear whether justice has been achieved.

Hamlet—a play about indecisiveness, and Hamlet's failure to act appropriately—is the most self-conscious tragedy. Shakespeare made it resonate with the most fundamental themes and problems of the Renaissance—a vast cultural phenomenon that began in the fifteenth-century Italy with the recovery of classical Greek and Latin texts that had been lost to the Middle Ages. The play is governed by the Renaissance atmosphere of art, ostentation, learning, and crime. The eponymous character himself is a renaissance scholar-prince—clever, melancholic, and introspective. Like a character in life itself, Hamlet may not be capable of full interpretation, though it is clear that through him Shakespeare explored the whole problem of action and reflective mind.

Renaissance humanism, as the movement is now called, generated a new interest in human experience, and also an enormous optimism about the potential scope of human understanding. Hamlet's famous speech in Act II, "What a piece of work is a man! How noble in reason, how infinite in faculty, in form and moving how express and admirable, in action how like an angel, in apprehension how like a god—the beauty of the world, the paragon of animals!" is directly based upon one of the major texts of the Italian humanists, Pico della Mirandola's *Oration on the Dignity of Man*. For the humanists, the purpose of cultivating reason was to lead to a better understanding of how to act, and their fondest hope was that the coordination of action and understanding would lead to great benefits for society as a whole.

Shakespeare allowed his characters a freedom to live their own lives to the uttermost confines of good and evil, but he was ever conscious that they existed in a moral world. The speeches in which Hamlet addresses the players show that Shakespeare felt the restriction of the actor's ability to interpret, and of the audience's intelligence in appreciation. He faced his contemporary audience, answered its needs, and contrived a drama which the Court could appreciate and the public enjoy. He wrote out the play fully as his own genius directed, knowing that deletion would be imperative when his script reached the theatre.

The world of other people is a world of appearances, and *Hamlet*, is fundamentally a play about the difficulty of living in that world.

THE CHARACTERS IN THE PLAY

Claudius, *King of Denmark*

Hamlet, *son to the late, and nephew to the present King*

Polonius, *Lord Chamberlain*

Horatio, *friend to Hamlet*

Laertes, *son to Polonius*

Voltimand, Cornelius, Rosencrantz, Guildenstern, Osric, a Gentleman, *courtiers*

A Priest

Marcellus, Barnardo, *officers*

Francisco, *a soldier*

Reynaldo, *servant to Polonius*

Players

Two Clowns, *grave-diggers*

Fortinbras, *Prince of Norway*

A Captain

English Ambassadors

Gertrude, *Queen of Denmark and mother to Hamlet*

Ophelia, *daughter to Polonius*

Lords, Ladies, Officers, Soldiers, Sailors, Messengers, and other Attendants

Ghost of Hamlet's Father

Act 1

SCENE: DENMARK

**SCENE I. ELSINORE.
A PLATFORM BEFORE THE CASTLE.**

FRANCISCO at his post. Enter to him BERNARDO

BERNARDO

Who's there?

FRANCISCO

Nay, answer me: stand, and unfold yourself.

BERNARDO

Long live the king!

FRANCISCO

Bernardo?

BERNARDO

He.

FRANCISCO

You come most carefully upon your hour.

BERNARDO

'Tis now struck twelve; get thee to bed,
Francisco.

FRANCISCO

For this relief much thanks: 'tis bitter cold,
And I am sick at heart.

BERNARDO

Have you had quiet guard?

FRANCISCO

Not a mouse stirring.

BERNARDO

Well, good night. If you do meet Horatio and
Marcellus,
The rivals of my watch, bid them make haste.

FRANCISCO

I think I hear them. Stand, ho! Who's there?

Enter HORATIO and MARCELLUS

HORATIO

Friends to this ground.

MARCELLUS

And liegemen to the Dane.

FRANCISCO

Give you good night.

MARCELLUS

O, farewell, honest soldier:
Who hath relieved you?

FRANCISCO

Bernardo has my place.

Give you good night.

Exit

MARCELLUS

Holla! Bernardo!

BERNARDO

Say, what, is Horatio there?

HORATIO

A piece of him.

BERNARDO

Welcome, Horatio, welcome, good Marcellus.

MARCELLUS

What, has this thing appear'd again to-night?

BERNARDO

I have seen nothing.

MARCELLUS

Horatio says 'tis but our fantasy,

And will not let belief take hold of him

Touching this dreaded sight, twice seen of us:

Therefore I have entreated him along

With us to watch the minutes of this night;

That if again this apparition come,

He may approve our eyes and speak to it.

HORATIO

Tush, tush, 'twill not appear.

BERNARDO

Sit down awhile;

And let us once again assail your ears,

That are so fortified against our story

What we have two nights seen.

HORATIO

Well, sit we down,

And let us hear Bernardo speak of this.

BERNARDO

Last night of all,

When yond same star that's westward from
the pole

Had made his course to illume that part of
heaven

Where now it burns, Marcellus and myself,

The bell then beating one—

Enter Ghost

MARCELLUS

Peace, break thee off; look, where it comes
again!

BERNARDO

In the same figure, like the king that's dead.

MARCELLUS

Thou art a scholar; speak to it, Horatio.

BERNARDO

Looks it not like the king? Mark it, Horatio.

HORATIO

Most like: it harrows me with fear and wonder.

BERNARDO

It would be spoke to.

MARCELLUS

Question it, Horatio.

HORATIO

What art thou that usurp'st this time of night,

Together with that fair and warlike form

In which the majesty of buried Denmark

Did sometimes march? by heaven I charge

thee, speak!

MARCELLUS

It is offended.

BERNARDO

See, it stalks away!

HORATIO

Stay! speak, speak! I charge thee, speak!

Exit Ghost

MARCELLUS

'Tis gone, and will not answer.

BERNARDO

How now, Horatio? You tremble and look pale:

Is not this something more than fantasy?

What think you on't?

HORATIO

Before my God, I might not this believe
Without the sensible and true avouch
Of mine own eyes.

MARCELLUS

Is it not like the king?

HORATIO

As thou art to thyself:
Such was the very armour he had on
When he the ambitious Norway combated;
So frown'd he once, when in an angry parle,
He smote the sledded Polacks on the ice.
'Tis strange.

MARCELLUS

Thus twice before, and jump at this dead hour,
With martial stalk hath he gone by our watch.

HORATIO

In what particular thought to work I know not;
But in the gross and scope of my opinion,
This bodes some strange eruption to our state.

MARCELLUS

Good now, sit down, and tell me, he that knows,
Why this same strict and most observant watch
So nightly toils the subject of the land,
And why such daily cast of brazen cannon,
And foreign mart for implements of war;

Why such impress of shipwrights, whose sore
    task
Does not divide the Sunday from the week;
What might be toward, that this sweaty haste
Doth make the night joint-labourer with the
    day:
Who is't that can inform me?

HORATIO
    That can I;
At least, the whisper goes so. Our last king,
Whose image even but now appear'd to us,
Was, as you know, by Fortinbras of Norway,
Thereto prick'd on by a most emulate pride,
Dared to the combat; in which our valiant
    Hamlet—
For so this side of our known world esteem'd
    him—
Did slay this Fortinbras; who by a seal'd compact,
Well ratified by law and heraldry,
Did forfeit, with his life, all those his lands
Which he stood seized of, to the conqueror:
Against the which, a moiety competent
Was gaged by our king; which had return'd
To the inheritance of Fortinbras,
Had he been vanquisher; as, by the same
    covenant,

And carriage of the article design'd,
His fell to Hamlet. Now, sir, young Fortinbras,
Of unimproved mettle hot and full,
Hath in the skirts of Norway here and there
Shark'd up a list of lawless resolutes,
For food and diet, to some enterprise
That hath a stomach in't; which is no other—
As it doth well appear unto our state—
But to recover of us, by strong hand
And terms compulsatory, those foresaid lands
So by his father lost: and this, I take it,
Is the main motive of our preparations,
The source of this our watch and the chief
    head
Of this post-haste and romage in the land.

BERNARDO

I think it be no other but e'en so:
Well may it sort that this portentous figure
Comes armed through our watch; so like the
    king
That was and is the question of these wars.

HORATIO

A mote it is to trouble the mind's eye.
In the most high and palmy state of Rome,
A little ere the mightiest Julius fell,
The graves stood tenantless and the sheeted
    dead

Did squeak and gibber in the Roman streets:
As stars with trains of fire and dews of blood,
Disasters in the sun; and the moist star
Upon whose influence Neptune's empire stands
Was sick almost to doomsday with eclipse:
And even the like precurse of fierce events,
As harbingers preceding still the fates
And prologue to the omen coming on,
Have heaven and earth together demonstrated
Unto our climatures and countrymen.
But soft, behold! lo, where it comes again!

Re-enter Ghost

I'll cross it, though it blast me. Stay, illusion!
If thou hast any sound, or use of voice,
Speak to me:
If there be any good thing to be done,
That may to thee do ease and grace to me,
Speak to me:

Cock crows

If thou art privy to thy country's fate,
Which, happily, foreknowing may avoid, O,
    speak!
Or if thou hast uphoarded in thy life
Extorted treasure in the womb of earth,

For which, they say, you spirits oft walk in
      death,
Speak of it: stay, and speak! Stop it, Marcellus.
MARCELLUS
Shall I strike at it with my partisan?
HORATIO
Do, if it will not stand.
BERNARDO
'Tis here!
HORATIO
'Tis here!
MARCELLUS
'Tis gone!

Exit Ghost

We do it wrong, being so majestical,
To offer it the show of violence;
For it is, as the air, invulnerable,
And our vain blows malicious mockery.
BERNARDO
It was about to speak, when the cock crew.
HORATIO
And then it started like a guilty thing
Upon a fearful summons. I have heard,
The cock, that is the trumpet to the morn,
Doth with his lofty and shrill-sounding throat
Awake the god of day; and, at his warning,
Whether in sea or fire, in earth or air,

The extravagant and erring spirit hies
To his confine: and of the truth herein
This present object made probation.

MARCELLUS

It faded on the crowing of the cock.
Some say that ever 'gainst that season comes
Wherein our Saviour's birth is celebrated,
The bird of dawning singeth all night long:
And then, they say, no spirit dares stir abroad;
The nights are wholesome; then no planets
    strike,
No fairy takes, nor witch hath power to charm,
So hallow'd and so gracious is the time.

HORATIO

So have I heard and do in part believe it.
But, look, the morn, in russet mantle clad,
Walks o'er the dew of yon high eastward hill:
Break we our watch up; and by my advice,
Let us impart what we have seen to-night
Unto young Hamlet; for, upon my life,
This spirit, dumb to us, will speak to him.
Do you consent we shall acquaint him with it,
As needful in our loves, fitting our duty?

MARCELLUS

Let's do't, I pray; and I this morning know
Where we shall find him most conveniently.

                              Exeunt

SCENE II. A ROOM OF STATE IN THE CASTLE.

Enter KING CLAUDIUS, QUEEN GERTRUDE, HAMLET, POLONIUS, LAERTES, VOLTIMAND, CORNELIUS, Lords, *and* Attendants

KING CLAUDIUS

    Though yet of Hamlet our dear brother's death
    The memory be green, and that it us befitted
    To bear our hearts in grief and our whole
        kingdom
    To be contracted in one brow of woe,
    Yet so far hath discretion fought with nature
    That we with wisest sorrow think on him,
    Together with remembrance of ourselves.
    Therefore our sometime sister, now our queen,
    The imperial jointress to this warlike state,
    Have we, as 'twere with a defeated joy,
    With an auspicious and a dropping eye,
    With mirth in funeral and with dirge in marriage,
    In equal scale weighing delight and dole,
    Taken to wife: nor have we herein barr'd
    Your better wisdoms, which have freely gone
    With this affair along. For all, our thanks.
    Now follows, that you know, young Fortinbras,
    Holding a weak supposal of our worth,

Or thinking by our late dear brother's death
Our state to be disjoint and out of frame,
Colleagued with the dream of his advantage,
He hath not fail'd to pester us with message,
Importing the surrender of those lands
Lost by his father, with all bonds of law,
To our most valiant brother. So much for him.
Now for ourself and for this time of meeting:
Thus much the business is: we have here writ
To Norway, uncle of young Fortinbras,
Who, impotent and bed-rid, scarcely hears
Of this his nephew's purpose, to suppress
His further gait herein; in that the levies,
The lists and full proportions, are all made
Out of his subject: and we here dispatch
You, good Cornelius, and you, Voltimand,
For bearers of this greeting to old Norway;
Giving to you no further personal power
To business with the king, more than the scope
Of these delated articles allow.
Farewell, and let your haste commend your
    duty.
CORNELIUS AND VOLTIMAND
In that and all things will we show our duty.
KING CLAUDIUS
We doubt it nothing: heartily farewell.
    Exeunt VOLTIMAND and CORNELIUS

And now, Laertes, what's the news with you?
You told us of some suit; what is't, Laertes?
You cannot speak of reason to the Dane,
And loose your voice: what wouldst thou beg,
    Laertes,
That shall not be my offer, not thy asking?
The head is not more native to the heart,
The hand more instrumental to the mouth,
Than is the throne of Denmark to thy father.
What wouldst thou have, Laertes?

LAERTES

My dread lord,
Your leave and favour to return to France;
From whence though willingly I came to
    Denmark,
To show my duty in your coronation,
Yet now, I must confess, that duty done,
My thoughts and wishes bend again toward
    France
And bow them to your gracious leave and
    pardon.

KING CLAUDIUS

Have you your father's leave? What says
Polonius?

LORD POLONIUS

He hath, my lord, wrung from me my slow
    leave

By laboursome petition, and at last
Upon his will I seal'd my hard consent:
I do beseech you, give him leave to go.
KING CLAUDIUS
Take thy fair hour, Laertes; time be thine,
And thy best graces spend it at thy will!
But now, my cousin Hamlet, and my son?
HAMLET
(Aside) A little more than kin, and less than
kind.
KING CLAUDIUS
How is it that the clouds still hang on you?
HAMLET
Not so, my lord; I am too much i' the sun.
QUEEN GERTRUDE
Good Hamlet, cast thy nighted colour off,
And let thine eye look like a friend on Denmark.
Do not for ever with thy vailed lids
Seek for thy noble father in the dust:
Thou know'st 'tis common; all that lives must
die,
Passing through nature to eternity.
HAMLET
Ay, madam, it is common.
QUEEN GERTRUDE
If it be,
Why seems it so particular with thee?

HAMLET

Seems, madam! nay it is; I know not 'seems.'
'Tis not alone my inky cloak, good mother,
Nor customary suits of solemn black,
Nor windy suspiration of forced breath,
No, nor the fruitful river in the eye,
Nor the dejected 'havior of the visage,
Together with all forms, moods, shapes of grief,
That can denote me truly: these indeed seem,
For they are actions that a man might play:
But I have that within which passeth show;
These but the trappings and the suits of woe.

KING CLAUDIUS

'Tis sweet and commendable in your nature,
    Hamlet,
To give these mourning duties to your father:
But, you must know, your father lost a father;
That father lost, lost his, and the survivor
    bound
In filial obligation for some term
To do obsequious sorrow: but to persever
In obstinate condolement is a course
Of impious stubbornness; 'tis unmanly grief;
It shows a will most incorrect to heaven,
A heart unfortified, a mind impatient,
An understanding simple and unschool'd:
For what we know must be and is as common

As any the most vulgar thing to sense,
Why should we in our peevish opposition
Take it to heart? Fie! 'tis a fault to heaven,
A fault against the dead, a fault to nature,
To reason most absurd: whose common theme
Is death of fathers, and who still hath cried,
From the first corse till he that died to-day,
'This must be so.' We pray you, throw to earth
This unprevailing woe, and think of us
As of a father: for let the world take note,
You are the most immediate to our throne;
And with no less nobility of love
Than that which dearest father bears his son,
Do I impart toward you. For your intent
In going back to school in Wittenberg,
It is most retrograde to our desire:
And we beseech you, bend you to remain
Here, in the cheer and comfort of our eye,
Our chiefest courtier, cousin, and our son.

QUEEN GERTRUDE

Let not thy mother lose her prayers, Hamlet:
I pray thee, stay with us; go not to Wittenberg.

HAMLET

I shall in all my best obey you, madam.

KING CLAUDIUS

Why, 'tis a loving and a fair reply:
Be as ourself in Denmark. Madam, come;

This gentle and unforced accord of Hamlet
Sits smiling to my heart: in grace whereof,
No jocund health that Denmark drinks to-day,
But the great cannon to the clouds shall tell,
And the king's rouse the heavens all bruit again,
Re-speaking earthly thunder. Come away.

Exeunt all but HAMLET

HAMLET
O, that this too too solid flesh would melt,
Thaw and resolve itself into a dew!
Or that the Everlasting had not fix'd
His canon 'gainst self-slaughter! O God! God!
How weary, stale, flat and unprofitable,
Seem to me all the uses of this world!
Fie on't! ah fie! 'tis an unweeded garden,
That grows to seed; things rank and gross in
    nature
Possess it merely. That it should come to this!
But two months dead: nay, not so much, not
    two:
So excellent a king; that was, to this,
Hyperion to a satyr; so loving to my mother
That he might not beteem the winds of heaven
Visit her face too roughly. Heaven and earth!
Must I remember? why, she would hang on
    him,

As if increase of appetite had grown
By what it fed on: and yet, within a month—
Let me not think on't—Frailty, thy name is
    woman!
A little month, or ere those shoes were old
With which she follow'd my poor father's body,
Like Niobe, all tears: why she, even she—
O, God! A beast that wants discourse of reason,
Would have mourn'd longer—married with my
    uncle,
My father's brother, but no more like my father
Than I to Hercules: within a month:
Ere yet the salt of most unrighteous tears
Had left the flushing in her galled eyes,
She married. O, most wicked speed, to post
With such dexterity to incestuous sheets!
It is not nor it cannot come to good:
But break, my heart; for I must hold my tongue.

Enter HORATIO, MARCELLUS, and BERNARDO
HORATIO
    Hail to your lordship!
HAMLET
    I am glad to see you well:
    Horatio, or I do forget myself.
HORATIO
    The same, my lord, and your poor servant ever.

HAMLET

> Sir, my good friend; I'll change that name
> with you:
> And what make you from Wittenberg, Horatio?
> Marcellus?

MARCELLUS

> My good lord—

HAMLET

> I am very glad to see you. Good even, sir.
> But what, in faith, make you from Wittenberg?

HORATIO

> A truant disposition, good my lord.

HAMLET

> I would not hear your enemy say so,
> Nor shall you do mine ear that violence,
> To make it truster of your own report
> Against yourself: I know you are no truant.
> But what is your affair in Elsinore?
> We'll teach you to drink deep ere you depart.

HORATIO

> My lord, I came to see your father's funeral.

HAMLET

> I pray thee, do not mock me, fellow-student;
> I think it was to see my mother's wedding.

HORATIO

> Indeed, my lord, it follow'd hard upon.

HAMLET

Thrift, thrift, Horatio! the funeral baked meats
Did coldly furnish forth the marriage tables.
Would I had met my dearest foe in heaven
Or ever I had seen that day, Horatio!
My father! methinks I see my father.

HORATIO

Where, my lord?

HAMLET

In my mind's eye, Horatio.

HORATIO

I saw him once; he was a goodly king.

HAMLET

He was a man, take him for all in all,
I shall not look upon his like again.

HORATIO

My lord, I think I saw him yesternight.

HAMLET

Saw? who?

HORATIO

My lord, the king your father.

HAMLET

The king my father!

HORATIO

Season your admiration for awhile
With an attent ear, till I may deliver,

Upon the witness of these gentlemen,
This marvel to you.

HAMLET

For God's love, let me hear.

HORATIO

Two nights together had these gentlemen,
Marcellus and Bernardo, on their watch,
In the dead vast and middle of the night,
Been thus encounter'd. A figure like your father,
Armed at point exactly, cap-a-pe,
Appears before them, and with solemn march
Goes slow and stately by them: thrice he walk'd
By their oppress'd and fear-surprised eyes,
Within his truncheon's length; whilst they, distilled
Almost to jelly with the act of fear,
Stand dumb and speak not to him. This to me
In dreadful secrecy impart they did;
And I with them the third night kept the watch;
Where, as they had deliver'd, both in time,
Form of the thing, each word made true and good,
The apparition comes: I knew your father;
These hands are not more like.

HAMLET

But where was this?

MARCELLUS

My lord, upon the platform where we watch'd.

HAMLET

Did you not speak to it?

HORATIO

My lord, I did;

But answer made it none: yet once methought

It lifted up its head and did address

Itself to motion, like as it would speak;

But even then the morning cock crew loud,

And at the sound it shrunk in haste away,

And vanish'd from our sight.

HAMLET

'Tis very strange.

HORATIO

As I do live, my honour'd lord, 'tis true;

And we did think it writ down in our duty

To let you know of it.

HAMLET

Indeed, indeed, sirs, but this troubles me.

Hold you the watch to-night?

MARCELLUS AND BERNARDO

We do, my lord.

HAMLET

Arm'd, say you?

MARCELLUS AND BERNARDO

Arm'd, my lord.

HAMLET

From top to toe?

MARCELLUS AND BERNARDO

My lord, from head to foot.

HAMLET

Then saw you not his face?

HORATIO

O, yes, my lord; he wore his beaver up.

HAMLET

What, look'd he frowningly?

HORATIO

A countenance more in sorrow than in anger.

HAMLET

Pale or red?

HORATIO

Nay, very pale.

HAMLET

And fix'd his eyes upon you?

HORATIO

Most constantly.

HAMLET

I would I had been there.

HORATIO

It would have much amazed you.

HAMLET

Very like, very like. Stay'd it long?

HORATIO

While one with moderate haste might tell a hundred.

MARCELLUS AND BERNARDO

Longer, longer.

HORATIO

Not when I saw't.

HAMLET

His beard was grizzled—no?

HORATIO

It was, as I have seen it in his life,
A sable silver'd.

HAMLET

I will watch to-night;
Perchance 'twill walk again.

HORATIO

I warrant it will.

HAMLET

If it assume my noble father's person,
I'll speak to it, though hell itself should gape
And bid me hold my peace. I pray you all,
If you have hitherto conceal'd this sight,
Let it be tenable in your silence still;
And whatsoever else shall hap to-night,
Give it an understanding, but no tongue:
I will requite your loves. So, fare you well:

Upon the platform, 'twixt eleven and twelve,
I'll visit you.

ALL

Our duty to your honour.

HAMLET

Your loves, as mine to you: farewell.

Exeunt all but HAMLET

My father's spirit in arms! all is not well;
I doubt some foul play: would the night
were come!
Till then sit still, my soul: foul deeds will rise,
Though all the earth o'erwhelm them, to
men's eyes.

Exit

SCENE III. A ROOM IN POLONIUS' HOUSE.

Enter LAERTES and OPHELIA

LAERTES

My necessaries are embark'd: farewell:
And, sister, as the winds give benefit
And convoy is assistant, do not sleep,
But let me hear from you.

OPHELIA

Do you doubt that?

LAERTES

> For Hamlet and the trifling of his favour,
> Hold it a fashion and a toy in blood,
> A violet in the youth of primy nature,
> Forward, not permanent, sweet, not lasting,
> The perfume and suppliance of a minute;
>> No more.

OPHELIA

> No more but so?

LAERTES

> Think it no more;
> For nature, crescent, does not grow alone
> In thews and bulk, but, as this temple waxes,
> The inward service of the mind and soul
> Grows wide withal. Perhaps he loves you now,
> And now no soil nor cautel doth besmirch
> The virtue of his will: but you must fear,
> His greatness weigh'd, his will is not his own;
> For he himself is subject to his birth:
> He may not, as unvalued persons do,
> Carve for himself; for on his choice depends
> The safety and health of this whole state;
> And therefore must his choice be circumscribed
> Unto the voice and yielding of that body
> Whereof he is the head. Then if he says he
>> loves you,

It fits your wisdom so far to believe it
As he in his particular act and place
May give his saying deed; which is no further
Than the main voice of Denmark goes withal.
Then weigh what loss your honour may sustain,
If with too credent ear you list his songs,
Or lose your heart, or your chaste treasure open
To his unmaster'd importunity.
Fear it, Ophelia, fear it, my dear sister,
And keep you in the rear of your affection,
Out of the shot and danger of desire.
The chariest maid is prodigal enough,
If she unmask her beauty to the moon:
Virtue itself 'scapes not calumnious strokes:
The canker galls the infants of the spring,
Too oft before their buttons be disclosed,
And in the morn and liquid dew of youth
Contagious blastments are most imminent.
Be wary then; best safety lies in fear:
Youth to itself rebels, though none else near.

OPHELIA

I shall the effect of this good lesson keep,
As watchman to my heart. But, good my
    brother,
Do not, as some ungracious pastors do,
Show me the steep and thorny way to heaven;
Whiles, like a puff'd and reckless libertine,

Himself the primrose path of dalliance treads,
And recks not his own rede.

LAERTES

O, fear me not.

I stay too long: but here my father comes.

Enter POLONIUS

A double blessing is a double grace,

Occasion smiles upon a second leave.

LORD POLONIUS

Yet here, Laertes! aboard, aboard, for shame!

The wind sits in the shoulder of your sail,

And you are stay'd for. There; my blessing with
   thee!

And these few precepts in thy memory

See thou character. Give thy thoughts no tongue,

Nor any unproportioned thought his act.

Be thou familiar, but by no means vulgar.

Those friends thou hast, and their adoption
   tried,

Grapple them to thy soul with hoops of steel;

But do not dull thy palm with entertainment

Of each new-hatch'd, unfledged comrade.
   Beware

Of entrance to a quarrel, but being in,

Bear't that the opposed may beware of thee.

Give every man thy ear, but few thy voice;

Take each man's censure, but reserve thy
    judgment.
Costly thy habit as thy purse can buy,
But not express'd in fancy; rich, not gaudy;
For the apparel oft proclaims the man,
And they in France of the best rank and station
Are of a most select and generous chief in that.
Neither a borrower nor a lender be;
For loan oft loses both itself and friend,
And borrowing dulls the edge of husbandry.
This above all: to thine ownself be true,
And it must follow, as the night the day,
Thou canst not then be false to any man.
Farewell: my blessing season this in thee!

LAERTES

Most humbly do I take my leave, my lord.

LORD POLONIUS

The time invites you; go; your servants tend.

LAERTES

Farewell, Ophelia; and remember well
What I have said to you.

OPHELIA

'Tis in my memory lock'd,
And you yourself shall keep the key of it.

LAERTES

Farewell.

Exit

LORD POLONIUS

What is't, Ophelia, be hath said to you?

OPHELIA

So please you, something touching the Lord
Hamlet.

LORD POLONIUS

Marry, well bethought:

'Tis told me, he hath very oft of late

Given private time to you; and you yourself

Have of your audience been most free and
bounteous:

If it be so, as so 'tis put on me,

And that in way of caution, I must tell you,

You do not understand yourself so clearly

As it behoves my daughter and your honour.

What is between you? give me up the truth.

OPHELIA

He hath, my lord, of late made many tenders
Of his affection to me.

LORD POLONIUS

Affection! pooh! you speak like a green girl,

Unsifted in such perilous circumstance.

Do you believe his tenders, as you call them?

OPHELIA

I do not know, my lord, what I should think.

LORD POLONIUS

Marry, I'll teach you: think yourself a baby;

That you have ta'en these tenders for true pay,
Which are not sterling. Tender yourself more
    dearly;
Or—not to crack the wind of the poor phrase,
Running it thus—you'll tender me a fool.
OPHELIA
My lord, he hath importuned me with love
In honourable fashion.
LORD POLONIUS
Ay, fashion you may call it; go to, go to.
OPHELIA
And hath given countenance to his speech,
    my lord,
With almost all the holy vows of heaven.
LORD POLONIUS
Ay, springes to catch woodcocks. I do know,
When the blood burns, how prodigal the soul
Lends the tongue vows: these blazes, daughter,
Giving more light than heat, extinct in both,
Even in their promise, as it is a-making,
You must not take for fire. From this time
Be somewhat scanter of your maiden presence;
Set your entreatments at a higher rate
Than a command to parley. For Lord Hamlet,
Believe so much in him, that he is young
And with a larger tether may he walk
Than may be given you: in few, Ophelia,

Do not believe his vows; for they are brokers,
Not of that dye which their investments show,
But mere implorators of unholy suits,
Breathing like sanctified and pious bawds,
The better to beguile. This is for all:
I would not, in plain terms, from this time forth,
Have you so slander any moment leisure,
As to give words or talk with the Lord Hamlet.
Look to't, I charge you: come your ways.

OPHELIA
I shall obey, my lord.

Exeunt

SCENE IV. THE PLATFORM.

Enter HAMLET, HORATIO, and MARCELLUS
HAMLET
The air bites shrewdly; it is very cold.
HORATIO
It is a nipping and an eager air.
HAMLET
What hour now?
HORATIO
I think it lacks of twelve.
HAMLET
No, it is struck.

HORATIO

Indeed? I heard it not: then it draws near the
season

Wherein the spirit held his wont to walk.

A flourish of trumpets, and ordnance shot off, within

What does this mean, my lord?

HAMLET

The king doth wake to-night and takes his
rouse,

Keeps wassail, and the swaggering up-spring
reels;

And, as he drains his draughts of Rhenish
down,

The kettle-drum and trumpet thus bray out

The triumph of his pledge.

HORATIO

Is it a custom?

HAMLET

Ay, marry, is't:

But to my mind, though I am native here

And to the manner born, it is a custom

More honour'd in the breach than the
observance.

This heavy-headed revel east and west

Makes us traduced and tax'd of other nations:

They clepe us drunkards, and with swinish
phrase

Soil our addition; and indeed it takes
From our achievements, though perform'd at
        height,
The pith and marrow of our attribute.
So, oft it chances in particular men,
That for some vicious mole of nature in them,
As, in their birth—wherein they are not guilty,
Since nature cannot choose his origin—
By the o'ergrowth of some complexion,
Oft breaking down the pales and forts of
        reason,
Or by some habit that too much o'er-leavens
The form of plausive manners, that these men,
Carrying, I say, the stamp of one defect,
Being nature's livery, or fortune's star,
Their virtues else be they as pure as grace,
As infinite as man may undergo—
Shall in the general censure take corruption
From that particular fault: the dram of eale
Doth all the noble substance of a doubt
To his own scandal.

HORATIO

Look, my lord, it comes!

Enter Ghost

HAMLET

Angels and ministers of grace defend us!

Be thou a spirit of health or goblin damn'd,
Bring with thee airs from heaven or blasts
     from hell,
Be thy intents wicked or charitable,
Thou comest in such a questionable shape
That I will speak to thee: I'll call thee Hamlet,
King, father, royal Dane: O, answer me!
Let me not burst in ignorance; but tell
Why thy canonized bones, hearsed in death,
Have burst their cerements; why the sepulchre,
Wherein we saw thee quietly inurn'd,
Hath oped his ponderous and marble jaws,
To cast thee up again. What may this mean,
That thou, dead corse, again in complete steel
Revisit'st thus the glimpses of the moon,
Making night hideous; and we fools of nature
So horridly to shake our disposition
With thoughts beyond the reaches of our souls?
Say, why is this? wherefore? what should we do?

Ghost beckons HAMLET

HORATIO
     It beckons you to go away with it,
     As if it some impartment did desire
     To you alone.

MARCELLUS

Look, with what courteous action

It waves you to a more removed ground:

But do not go with it.

HORATIO

No, by no means.

HAMLET

It will not speak; then I will follow it.

HORATIO

Do not, my lord.

HAMLET

Why, what should be the fear?

I do not set my life in a pin's fee;

And for my soul, what can it do to that,

Being a thing immortal as itself?

It waves me forth again: I'll follow it.

HORATIO

What if it tempt you toward the flood, my lord,

Or to the dreadful summit of the cliff

That beetles o'er his base into the sea,

And there assume some other horrible form,

Which might deprive your sovereignty of reason

And draw you into madness? think of it:

The very place puts toys of desperation,

Without more motive, into every brain

That looks so many fathoms to the sea

And hears it roar beneath.

HAMLET

It waves me still.

Go on; I'll follow thee.

MARCELLUS

You shall not go, my lord.

HAMLET

Hold off your hands.

HORATIO

Be ruled; you shall not go.

HAMLET

My fate cries out,

And makes each petty artery in this body

As hardy as the Nemean lion's nerve.

Still am I call'd. Unhand me, gentlemen.

By heaven, I'll make a ghost of him that
lets me!

I say, away! Go on; I'll follow thee.

Exeunt Ghost and HAMLET

HORATIO

He waxes desperate with imagination.

MARCELLUS

Let's follow; 'tis not fit thus to obey him.

HORATIO

Have after. To what issue will this come?

MARCELLUS

Something is rotten in the state of Denmark.

HORATIO

Heaven will direct it.

MARCELLUS

Nay, let's follow him.

Exeunt

SCENE V. ANOTHER PART OF THE PLATFORM.

Enter GHOST and HAMLET

HAMLET

Where wilt thou lead me? speak; I'll go no further.

GHOST

Mark me.

HAMLET

I will.

GHOST

My hour is almost come,
When I to sulphurous and tormenting flames
Must render up myself.

HAMLET

Alas, poor ghost!

GHOST

Pity me not, but lend thy serious hearing
To what I shall unfold.

HAMLET
     Speak; I am bound to hear.
GHOST
     So art thou to revenge, when thou shalt hear.
HAMLET
     What?
GHOST
     I am thy father's spirit,
     Doom'd for a certain term to walk the night,
     And for the day confined to fast in fires,
     Till the foul crimes done in my days of nature
     Are burnt and purged away. But that I am forbid
     To tell the secrets of my prison-house,
     I could a tale unfold whose lightest word
     Would harrow up thy soul, freeze thy young
          blood,
     Make thy two eyes, like stars, start from their
          spheres,
     Thy knotted and combined locks to part
     And each particular hair to stand on end,
     Like quills upon the fretful porpentine:
     But this eternal blazon must not be
     To ears of flesh and blood. List, list, O, list!
     If thou didst ever thy dear father love—
HAMLET
     O God!

GHOST
> Revenge his foul and most unnatural murder.

HAMLET
> Murder!

GHOST
> Murder most foul, as in the best it is;
> But this most foul, strange and unnatural.

HAMLET
> Haste me to know't, that I, with wings as swift
> As meditation or the thoughts of love,
> May sweep to my revenge.

GHOST
> I find thee apt;
> And duller shouldst thou be than the fat weed
> That roots itself in ease on Lethe wharf,
> Wouldst thou not stir in this. Now, Hamlet, hear:
> 'Tis given out that, sleeping in my orchard,
> A serpent stung me; so the whole ear of Denmark
> Is by a forged process of my death
> Rankly abused: but know, thou noble youth,
> The serpent that did sting thy father's life
> Now wears his crown.

HAMLET
> O my prophetic soul! My uncle!

GHOST

    Ay, that incestuous, that adulterate beast,
    With witchcraft of his wit, with traitorous
        gifts—
    O wicked wit and gifts, that have the power
    So to seduce!—won to his shameful lust
    The will of my most seeming-virtuous queen:
    O Hamlet, what a falling-off was there!
    From me, whose love was of that dignity
    That it went hand in hand even with the vow
    I made to her in marriage, and to decline
    Upon a wretch whose natural gifts were poor
    To those of mine!
    But virtue, as it never will be moved,
    Though lewdness court it in a shape of heaven,
    So lust, though to a radiant angel link’d,
    Will sate itself in a celestial bed,
    And prey on garbage.
    But, soft! methinks I scent the morning air;
    Brief let me be. Sleeping within my orchard,
    My custom always of the afternoon,
    Upon my secure hour thy uncle stole,
    With juice of cursed hebenon in a vial,
    And in the porches of my ears did pour
    The leperous distilment; whose effect
    Holds such an enmity with blood of man
    That swift as quicksilver it courses through

The natural gates and alleys of the body,
And with a sudden vigour doth posset
And curd, like eager droppings into milk,
The thin and wholesome blood: so did it mine;
And a most instant tetter bark'd about,
Most lazar-like, with vile and loathsome crust,
All my smooth body.
Thus was I, sleeping, by a brother's hand
Of life, of crown, of queen, at once dispatch'd:
Cut off even in the blossoms of my sin,
Unhousel'd, disappointed, unanel'd,
No reckoning made, but sent to my account
With all my imperfections on my head:
O, horrible! O, horrible! most horrible!
If thou hast nature in thee, bear it not;
Let not the royal bed of Denmark be
A couch for luxury and damned incest.
But, howsoever thou pursuest this act,
Taint not thy mind, nor let thy soul contrive
Against thy mother aught: leave her to heaven
And to those thorns that in her bosom lodge,
To prick and sting her. Fare thee well at once!
The glow-worm shows the matin to be near,
And 'gins to pale his uneffectual fire:
Adieu, adieu! Hamlet, remember me.

Exit

HAMLET

O all you host of heaven! O earth! what else?
And shall I couple hell? O, fie! Hold, hold, my
    heart;
And you, my sinews, grow not instant old,
But bear me stiffly up. Remember thee!
Ay, thou poor ghost, while memory holds a seat
In this distracted globe. Remember thee!
Yea, from the table of my memory
I'll wipe away all trivial fond records,
All saws of books, all forms, all pressures past,
That youth and observation copied there;
And thy commandment all alone shall live
Within the book and volume of my brain,
Unmix'd with baser matter: yes, by heaven!
O most pernicious woman!
O villain, villain, smiling, damned villain!
My tables, meet it is I set it down,
That one may smile, and smile, and be a villain;
At least I'm sure it may be so in Denmark:
Writing
So, uncle, there you are. Now to my word;
It is 'Adieu, adieu! remember me.'
I have sworn 't.

MARCELLUS AND HORATIO

(Within) My lord, my lord—

MARCELLUS

(Within) Lord Hamlet—

HORATIO

(Within) Heaven secure him!

HAMLET

So be it!

HORATIO

(Within) Hillo, ho, ho, my lord!

HAMLET

Hillo, ho, ho, boy! come, bird, come.

Enter HORATIO and MARCELLUS

MARCELLUS

How is't, my noble lord?

HORATIO

What news, my lord?

HAMLET

O, wonderful!

HORATIO

Good my lord, tell it.

HAMLET

No; you'll reveal it.

HORATIO

Not I, my lord, by heaven.

MARCELLUS

Nor I, my lord.

HAMLET

How say you, then; would heart of man once
think it?

But you'll be secret?

HORATIO AND MARCELLUS

Ay, by heaven, my lord.

HAMLET

There's ne'er a villain dwelling in all Denmark
But he's an arrant knave.

HORATIO

There needs no ghost, my lord, come from the
grave
To tell us this.

HAMLET

Why, right; you are i' the right;
And so, without more circumstance at all,
I hold it fit that we shake hands and part:
You, as your business and desire shall point you;
For every man has business and desire,
Such as it is; and for mine own poor part,
Look you, I'll go pray.

HORATIO

These are but wild and whirling words, my
lord.

HAMLET

I'm sorry they offend you, heartily;
Yes, faith heartily.

HORATIO

There's no offence, my lord.

HAMLET

Yes, by Saint Patrick, but there is, Horatio,

And much offence too. Touching this vision
here,

It is an honest ghost, that let me tell you:

For your desire to know what is between us,

O'ermaster 't as you may. And now, good friends,

As you are friends, scholars and soldiers,

Give me one poor request.

HORATIO

What is't, my lord? we will.

HAMLET

Never make known what you have seen to-
night.

HORATIO AND MARCELLUS

My lord, we will not.

HAMLET

Nay, but swear't.

HORATIO

In faith,

My lord, not I.

MARCELLUS

Nor I, my lord, in faith.

HAMLET

Upon my sword.

MARCELLUS

We have sworn, my lord, already.

HAMLET

Indeed, upon my sword, indeed.

GHOST

(Beneath) Swear.

HAMLET

Ah, ha, boy! say'st thou so?

art thou there, truepenny?

Come on—you hear this fellow in the
cellarage—

Consent to swear.

HORATIO

Propose the oath, my lord.

HAMLET

Never to speak of this that you have seen,

Swear by my sword.

GHOST

(Beneath) Swear.

HAMLET

Hic et ubique? Then we'll shift our ground.

Come hither, gentlemen,

And lay your hands again upon my sword:

Never to speak of this that you have heard,

Swear by my sword.

GHOST

(Beneath) Swear.

HAMLET

> Well said, old mole! canst work i' the earth so
> fast?
> A worthy pioner! Once more remove, good
> friends.

HORATIO

> O day and night, but this is wondrous strange!

HAMLET

> And therefore as a stranger give it welcome.
> There are more things in heaven and earth,
> Horatio,
> Than are dreamt of in your philosophy. But
> come;
> Here, as before, never, so help you mercy,
> How strange or odd soe'er I bear myself,
> As I perchance hereafter shall think meet
> To put an antic disposition on,
> That you, at such times seeing me, never shall,
> With arms encumber'd thus, or this headshake,
> Or by pronouncing of some doubtful phrase,
> As 'Well, well, we know,' or 'We could, an if we
> would,'
> Or 'If we list to speak,' or 'There be, an if they
> might,'
> Or such ambiguous giving out, to note
> That you know aught of me: this not to do,

So grace and mercy at your most need help you,
    Swear.
GHOST
    (Beneath) Swear.
HAMLET
    Rest, rest, perturbed spirit!
    They swear
    So, gentlemen,
    With all my love I do commend me to you:
    And what so poor a man as Hamlet is
    May do, to express his love and friending to
        you,
    God willing, shall not lack. Let us go in together;
    And still your fingers on your lips, I pray.
    The time is out of joint: O cursed spite,
    That ever I was born to set it right!
    Nay, come, let's go together.

Exeunt

Act 2

SCENE I. A ROOM IN POLONIUS' HOUSE.

Enter POLONIUS and REYNALDO

LORD POLONIUS

Give him this money and these notes, Reynaldo.

REYNALDO

I will, my lord.

LORD POLONIUS

You shall do marvellous wisely, good Reynaldo,
Before you visit him, to make inquire
Of his behavior.

REYNALDO

My lord, I did intend it.

LORD POLONIUS

Marry, well said; very well said. Look you, sir,
Inquire me first what Danskers are in Paris;

And how, and who, what means, and where
    they keep,
What company, at what expense; and finding
By this encompassment and drift of question
That they do know my son, come you more
    nearer
Than your particular demands will touch it:
Take you, as 'twere, some distant knowledge
    of him;
As thus, 'I know his father and his friends,
And in part him.' Do you mark this, Reynaldo?
REYNALDO
    Ay, very well, my lord.
LORD POLONIUS
    'And in part him; but' you may say 'not well:
    But, if't be he I mean, he's very wild;
    Addicted so and so:' and there put on him
    What forgeries you please; marry, none so rank
    As may dishonour him; take heed of that;
    But, sir, such wanton, wild and usual slips
    As are companions noted and most known
    To youth and liberty.
REYNALDO
    As gaming, my lord.
LORD POLONIUS
    Ay, or drinking, fencing, swearing, quarrelling,
    Drabbing: you may go so far.

REYNALDO

> My lord, that would dishonour him.

LORD POLONIUS

> Faith, no; as you may season it in the charge
> You must not put another scandal on him,
> That he is open to incontinency;
> That's not my meaning:
> but breathe his faults so quaintly
> That they may seem the taints of liberty,
> The flash and outbreak of a fiery mind,
> A savageness in unreclaimed blood,
> Of general assault.

REYNALDO

> But, my good lord—

LORD POLONIUS

> Wherefore should you do this?

REYNALDO

> Ay, my lord,
> I would know that.

LORD POLONIUS

> Marry, sir, here's my drift;
> And I believe, it is a fetch of wit:
> You laying these slight sullies on my son,
> As 'twere a thing a little soil'd i' the working,
> Mark you,
> Your party in converse, him you would sound,
> Having ever seen in the prenominate crimes

The youth you breathe of guilty, be assured
He closes with you in this consequence;
'Good sir,' or so, or 'friend,' or 'gentleman,'
According to the phrase or the addition
Of man and country.
REYNALDO
Very good, my lord.
LORD POLONIUS
And then, sir, does he this—he does—what
was I about to say? By the mass, I was about to
say something: where did I leave?
REYNALDO
At 'closes in the consequence,'
at 'friend or so,' and 'gentleman.'
LORD POLONIUS
At 'closes in the consequence,' ay, marry;
He closes thus: 'I know the gentleman;
I saw him yesterday, or t' other day,
Or then, or then; with such, or such; and, as
        you say,
There was a' gaming; there o'ertook in's rouse;
There falling out at tennis:' or perchance,
'I saw him enter such a house of sale,'
Videlicet, a brothel, or so forth.
See you now;
Your bait of falsehood takes this carp of truth:
And thus do we of wisdom and of reach,

With windlasses and with assays of bias,
By indirections find directions out:
So by my former lecture and advice,
Shall you my son. You have me, have you not?

REYNALDO

My lord, I have.

LORD POLONIUS

God be wi' you; fare you well.

REYNALDO

Good my lord!

LORD POLONIUS

Observe his inclination in yourself.

REYNALDO

I shall, my lord.

LORD POLONIUS

And let him ply his music.

REYNALDO

Well, my lord.

LORD POLONIUS

Farewell!

Exit REYNALDO

Enter OPHELIA

How now, Ophelia! What's the matter?

OPHELIA

O, my lord, my lord, I have been so affrighted!

LORD POLONIUS

    With what, i' the name of God?

OPHELIA

    My lord, as I was sewing in my closet,
    Lord Hamlet, with his doublet all unbraced;
    No hat upon his head; his stockings foul'd,
    Ungarter'd, and down-gyved to his ancle;
    Pale as his shirt; his knees knocking each other;
    And with a look so piteous in purport
    As if he had been loosed out of hell
    To speak of horrors—he comes before me.

LORD POLONIUS

    Mad for thy love?

OPHELIA

    My lord, I do not know;
    But truly, I do fear it.

LORD POLONIUS

    What said he?

OPHELIA

    He took me by the wrist and held me hard;
    Then goes he to the length of all his arm;
    And, with his other hand thus o'er his brow,
    He falls to such perusal of my face
    As he would draw it. Long stay'd he so;
    At last, a little shaking of mine arm
    And thrice his head thus waving up and down,
    He raised a sigh so piteous and profound

As it did seem to shatter all his bulk
And end his being: that done, he lets me go:
And, with his head over his shoulder turn'd,
He seem'd to find his way without his eyes;
For out o' doors he went without their helps,
And, to the last, bended their light on me.

LORD POLONIUS

Come, go with me: I will go seek the king.
This is the very ecstasy of love,
Whose violent property fordoes itself
And leads the will to desperate undertakings
As oft as any passion under heaven
That does afflict our natures. I am sorry.
What, have you given him any hard words
    of late?

OPHELIA

No, my good lord, but, as you did command,
I did repel his fetters and denied
His access to me.

LORD POLONIUS

That hath made him mad.
I am sorry that with better heed and judgment
I had not quoted him: I fear'd he did but trifle,
And meant to wreck thee; but, beshrew my
    jealousy!
By heaven, it is as proper to our age
To cast beyond ourselves in our opinions

As it is common for the younger sort
To lack discretion. Come, go we to the king:
This must be known; which,
being kept close, might move
More grief to hide than hate to utter love.

Exeunt

SCENE II. A ROOM IN THE CASTLE.

Enter KING CLAUDIUS, QUEEN GERTRUDE, ROSENCRANTZ, GUILDENSTERN, and attendants

KING CLAUDIUS

Welcome, dear Rosencrantz and Guildenstern!
Moreover that we much did long to see you,
The need we have to use you did provoke
Our hasty sending. Something have you heard
Of Hamlet's transformation; so call it,
Sith nor the exterior nor the inward man
Resembles that it was. What it should be,
More than his father's death, that thus hath
    put him
So much from the understanding of himself,
I cannot dream of: I entreat you both,
That, being of so young days brought up with
    him,
And sith so neighbour'd to his youth and havior,

That you vouchsafe your rest here in our court
Some little time: so by your companies
To draw him on to pleasures, and to gather,
So much as from occasion you may glean,
Whether aught, to us unknown, afflicts him thus,
That, open'd, lies within our remedy.

QUEEN GERTRUDE

Good gentlemen, he hath much talk'd of you;
And sure I am two men there are not living
To whom he more adheres. If it will please you
To show us so much gentry and good will
As to expend your time with us awhile,
For the supply and profit of our hope,
Your visitation shall receive such thanks
As fits a king's remembrance.

ROSENCRANTZ

Both your majesties
Might, by the sovereign power you have of us,
Put your dread pleasures more into command
Than to entreaty.

GUILDENSTERN

But we both obey,
And here give up ourselves, in the full bent
To lay our service freely at your feet,
To be commanded.

KING CLAUDIUS

Thanks, Rosencrantz and gentle Guildenstern.

QUEEN GERTRUDE

Thanks, Guildenstern and gentle Rosencrantz:
And I beseech you instantly to visit
My too much changed son. Go, some of you,
And bring these gentlemen where Hamlet is.

GUILDENSTERN

Heavens make our presence and our practises
Pleasant and helpful to him!

QUEEN GERTRUDE

Ay, amen!

*Exeunt ROSENCRANTZ,
GUILDENSTERN, and some Attendants*

Enter POLONIUS

LORD POLONIUS

The ambassadors from Norway, my good lord,
Are joyfully return'd.

KING CLAUDIUS

Thou still hast been the father of good news.

LORD POLONIUS

Have I, my lord? I assure my good liege,
I hold my duty, as I hold my soul,
Both to my God and to my gracious king:
And I do think, or else this brain of mine
Hunts not the trail of policy so sure
As it hath used to do, that I have found
The very cause of Hamlet's lunacy.

KING CLAUDIUS

O, speak of that; that do I long to hear.

LORD POLONIUS

Give first admittance to the ambassadors;

My news shall be the fruit to that great feast.

KING CLAUDIUS

Thyself do grace to them, and bring them in.

Exit POLONIUS

He tells me, my dear Gertrude, he hath found

The head and source of all your son's distemper.

QUEEN GERTRUDE

I doubt it is no other but the main;

His father's death, and our o'erhasty marriage.

KING CLAUDIUS

Well, we shall sift him.

Re-enter POLONIUS, with VOLTIMAND and CORNELIUS

Welcome, my good friends!

Say, Voltimand, what from our brother Norway?

VOLTIMAND

Most fair return of greetings and desires.

Upon our first, he sent out to suppress

His nephew's levies; which to him appear'd

To be a preparation 'gainst the Polack;

But, better look'd into, he truly found

It was against your highness: whereat grieved,
That so his sickness, age and impotence
Was falsely borne in hand, sends out arrests
On Fortinbras; which he, in brief, obeys;
Receives rebuke from Norway, and in fine
Makes vow before his uncle never more
To give the assay of arms against your majesty.
Whereon old Norway, overcome with joy,
Gives him three thousand crowns in annual fee,
And his commission to employ those soldiers,
So levied as before, against the Polack:
With an entreaty, herein further shown,

Giving a paper

That it might please you to give quiet pass
Through your dominions for this enterprise,
On such regards of safety and allowance
As therein are set down.

KING CLAUDIUS

It likes us well;
And at our more consider'd time well read,
Answer, and think upon this business.
Meantime we thank you for your well-took
     labour:
Go to your rest; at night we'll feast together:
Most welcome home!

Exeunt VOLTIMAND and CORNELIUS

LORD POLONIUS

    This business is well ended.

    My liege, and madam, to expostulate

    What majesty should be, what duty is,

    Why day is day, night night, and time is time,

    Were nothing but to waste night, day and time.

    Therefore, since brevity is the soul of wit,

    And tediousness the limbs and outward

        flourishes,

    I will be brief: your noble son is mad:

    Mad call I it; for, to define true madness,

    What is't but to be nothing else but mad?

    But let that go.

QUEEN GERTRUDE

    More matter, with less art.

LORD POLONIUS

    Madam, I swear I use no art at all.

    That he is mad, 'tis true: 'tis true 'tis pity;

    And pity 'tis 'tis true: a foolish figure;

    But farewell it, for I will use no art.

    Mad let us grant him, then: and now remains

    That we find out the cause of this effect,

    Or rather say, the cause of this defect,

    For this effect defective comes by cause:

    Thus it remains, and the remainder thus.

        Perpend.

    I have a daughter—have while she is mine—

Who, in her duty and obedience, mark,
Hath given me this: now gather, and surmise.
Reads
'To the celestial and my soul's idol, the most
    beautified Ophelia,'—
That's an ill phrase, a vile phrase; 'beautified' is
    a vile phrase: but you shall hear. Thus:
Reads
'In her excellent white bosom, these, & c.'
QUEEN GERTRUDE
Came this from Hamlet to her?
LORD POLONIUS
Good madam, stay awhile; I will be faithful.
Reads
'Doubt thou the stars are fire;
Doubt that the sun doth move;
Doubt truth to be a liar;
But never doubt I love.
'O dear Ophelia, I am ill at these numbers;
I have not art to reckon my groans: but that
I love thee best, O most best, believe it. Adieu.
'Thine evermore most dear lady, whilst
this machine is to him, HAMLET.'
This, in obedience, hath my daughter shown me,
And more above, hath his solicitings,
As they fell out by time, by means and place,
All given to mine ear.

KING CLAUDIUS
  But how hath she
  Received his love?
LORD POLONIUS
  What do you think of me?
KING CLAUDIUS
  As of a man faithful and honourable.
LORD POLONIUS
  I would fain prove so. But what might you
      think,
  When I had seen this hot love on the wing—
  As I perceived it, I must tell you that,
  Before my daughter told me—what might you,
  Or my dear majesty your queen here, think,
  If I had play'd the desk or table-book,
  Or given my heart a winking, mute and dumb,
  Or look'd upon this love with idle sight;
  What might you think? No, I went round to
      work,
  And my young mistress thus I did bespeak:
  'Lord Hamlet is a prince, out of thy star;
  This must not be:' and then I precepts gave her,
  That she should lock herself from his resort,
  Admit no messengers, receive no tokens.
  Which done, she took the fruits of my advice;
  And he, repulsed—a short tale to make—
  Fell into a sadness, then into a fast,

Thence to a watch, thence into a weakness,
Thence to a lightness, and, by this declension,
Into the madness wherein now he raves,
And all we mourn for.
KING CLAUDIUS
Do you think 'tis this?
QUEEN GERTRUDE
It may be, very likely.
LORD POLONIUS
Hath there been such a time—I'd fain know
    that—
That I have positively said 'Tis so,
When it proved otherwise?
KING CLAUDIUS
Not that I know.
LORD POLONIUS
(Pointing to his head and shoulder)
Take this from this, if this be otherwise:
If circumstances lead me, I will find
Where truth is hid, though it were hid indeed
Within the centre.
KING CLAUDIUS
How may we try it further?
LORD POLONIUS
You know, sometimes he walks four hours
    together
Here in the lobby.

QUEEN GERTRUDE

    So he does indeed.

LORD POLONIUS

    At such a time I'll loose my daughter to him:

    Be you and I behind an arras then;

    Mark the encounter: if he love her not

    And be not from his reason fall'n thereon,

    Let me be no assistant for a state,

    But keep a farm and carters.

KING CLAUDIUS

    We will try it.

QUEEN GERTRUDE

    But, look, where sadly the poor wretch comes

    reading.

LORD POLONIUS

    Away, I do beseech you, both away:

    I'll board him presently.

                Exeunt KING CLAUDIUS, QUEEN

                       GERTRUDE, and Attendants

Enter HAMLET, reading

    O, give me leave:

    How does my good Lord Hamlet?

HAMLET

    Well, God-a-mercy.

LORD POLONIUS

    Do you know me, my lord?

HAMLET

Excellent well; you are a fishmonger.

LORD POLONIUS

Not I, my lord.

HAMLET

Then I would you were so honest a man.

LORD POLONIUS

Honest, my lord!

HAMLET

Ay, sir; to be honest, as this world goes, is to be one man picked out of ten thousand.

LORD POLONIUS

That's very true, my lord.

HAMLET

For if the sun breed maggots in a dead dog, being a god kissing carrion,—Have you a daughter?

LORD POLONIUS

I have, my lord.

HAMLET

Let her not walk i' the sun: conception is a blessing: but not as your daughter may conceive. Friend, look to 't.

LORD POLONIUS

(Aside) How say you by that? Still harping on my daughter: yet he knew me not at first; he said I was a fishmonger: he is far gone, far gone: and truly in my youth I suffered much extremity for love; very near this. I'll speak to him again. What do you read, my lord?

HAMLET

Words, words, words.

LORD POLONIUS

What is the matter, my lord?

HAMLET

Between who?

LORD POLONIUS

I mean, the matter that you read, my lord.

HAMLET

Slanders, sir: for the satirical rogue says here that old men have grey beards, that their faces are wrinkled, their eyes purging thick amber and plum tree gum and that they have a plentiful lack of wit, together with most weak hams: all which, sir, though I most powerfully and potently believe, yet I hold it not honesty to have it thus set down, for yourself, sir, should be old as I am, if like a crab you could go backward.

LORD POLONIUS

(Aside) Though this be madness, yet there is method in 't. Will you walk out of the air, my lord?

HAMLET

Into my grave.

LORD POLONIUS

Indeed, that is out o' the air.

Aside

How pregnant sometimes his replies are! a happiness that often madness hits on, which reason and sanity could not so prosperously be delivered of. I will leave him, and suddenly contrive the means of meeting between him and my daughter. My honourable lord, I will most humbly take my leave of you.

HAMLET

You cannot, sir, take from me any thing that I will more willingly part withal: except my life, except my life, except my life.

LORD POLONIUS

Fare you well, my lord.

HAMLET

These tedious old fools!

Enter ROSENCRANTZ and GUILDENSTERN

LORD POLONIUS

You go to seek the Lord Hamlet; there he is.

ROSENCRANTZ

(To POLONIUS) God save you, sir!

Exit POLONIUS

GUILDENSTERN

My honoured lord!

ROSENCRANTZ

My most dear lord!

HAMLET

My excellent good friends! How dost thou,
Guildenstern? Ah, Rosencrantz! Good lads,
how do ye both?

ROSENCRANTZ

As the indifferent children of the earth.

GUILDENSTERN

Happy, in that we are not over-happy;
On fortune's cap we are not the very button.

HAMLET

Nor the soles of her shoe?

ROSENCRANTZ

Neither, my lord.

HAMLET

Then you live about her waist,
or in the middle of her favours?

GUILDENSTERN

Faith, her privates we.

HAMLET

In the secret parts of fortune? O, most true;
she is a strumpet. What's the news?

ROSENCRANTZ

None, my lord, but that the world's grown honest.

HAMLET

Then is doomsday near: but your news is not true. Let me question more in particular: what have you, my good friends, deserved at the hands of fortune, that she sends you to prison hither?

GUILDENSTERN

Prison, my lord!

HAMLET

Denmark's a prison.

ROSENCRANTZ

Then is the world one.

HAMLET

A goodly one; in which there are many confines, wards and dungeons, Denmark being one o' the worst.

ROSENCRANTZ

We think not so, my lord.

HAMLET

Why, then, 'tis none to you; for there is nothing either good or bad, but thinking makes it so: to me it is a prison.

ROSENCRANTZ

Why then, your ambition makes it one; 'tis too narrow for your mind.

HAMLET

O God, I could be bounded in a nut shell and count myself a king of infinite space, were it not that I have bad dreams.

GUILDENSTERN

Which dreams indeed are ambition, for the very substance of the ambitious is merely the shadow of a dream.

HAMLET

A dream itself is but a shadow.

ROSENCRANTZ

Truly, and I hold ambition of so airy and light a quality that it is but a shadow's shadow.

HAMLET

Then are our beggars bodies, and our monarchs and outstretched heroes the beggars' shadows. Shall we to the court? for, by my fay, I cannot reason.

ROSENCRANTZ AND GUILDENSTERN

We'll wait upon you.

HAMLET

No such matter: I will not sort you with the rest of my servants, for, to speak to you like an honest man, I am most dreadfully attended. But, in the beaten way of friendship, what make you at Elsinore?

ROSENCRANTZ

To visit you, my lord; no other occasion.

HAMLET

Beggar that I am, I am even poor in thanks; but I thank you: and sure, dear friends, my thanks are too dear a halfpenny. Were you not sent for? Is it your own inclining? Is it a free visitation? Come, deal justly with me: come, come; nay, speak.

GUILDENSTERN

What should we say, my lord?

HAMLET

Why, any thing, but to the purpose. You were sent for; and there is a kind of confession in your looks which your modesties have not craft enough to colour: I know the good king and queen have sent for you.

ROSENCRANTZ

To what end, my lord?

HAMLET

That you must teach me. But let me conjure you, by the rights of our fellowship, by the consonancy of our youth, by the obligation of our ever-preserved love, and by what more dear a better proposer could charge you withal, be even and direct with me, whether you were sent for, or no?

ROSENCRANTZ

(Aside to GUILDENSTERN) What say you?

HAMLET

(Aside) Nay, then, I have an eye of you. If you love me, hold not off.

GUILDENSTERN

My lord, we were sent for.

HAMLET

I will tell you why; so shall my anticipation prevent your discovery, and your secrecy to the king and queen moult no feather. I have of late—but wherefore I know not—lost all my mirth, forgone all custom of exercises; and indeed it goes so heavily with my disposition that this goodly frame, the earth, seems to me a sterile promontory, this most excellent canopy, the air, look you, this brave o'erhanging firmament, this majestical roof fretted with golden fire, why, it appears no other thing to me than a foul and pestilent congregation of vapours. What a piece of work is a man! how noble in reason! how infinite in faculty! in form and moving how express and admirable! in action how like an angel! in apprehension how like a god! the beauty of the world! the paragon of animals! And yet, to me, what is this quintessence of dust? man delights not me: no, nor woman neither, though by your smiling you seem to say so.

ROSENCRANTZ

My lord, there was no such stuff in my thoughts.

HAMLET

Why did you laugh then, when I said 'man delights not me'?

ROSENCRANTZ

To think, my lord, if you delight not in man, what lenten entertainment the players shall receive from you: we coted them on the way; and hither are they coming, to offer you service.

HAMLET

He that plays the king shall be welcome; his majesty shall have tribute of me; the adventurous knight shall use his foil and target; the lover shall not sigh gratis; the humourous man shall end his part in peace; the clown shall make those laugh whose lungs are tickled o' the sere; and the lady shall say her mind freely, or the blank verse shall halt for't. What players are they?

ROSENCRANTZ

Even those you were wont to take delight in, the tragedians of the city.

HAMLET

How chances it they travel? their residence,
both in reputation and profit, was better both
ways.

ROSENCRANTZ

I think their inhibition comes by the means of
the late innovation.

HAMLET

Do they hold the same estimation they did
when I was in the city? are they so followed?

ROSENCRANTZ

No, indeed, are they not.

HAMLET

How comes it? do they grow rusty?

ROSENCRANTZ

Nay, their endeavour keeps in the wonted
pace: but there is, sir, an aery of children, little
eyases, that cry out on the top of question, and
are most tyrannically clapped for't: these are
now the fashion, and so berattle the common
stages—so they call them—that many wearing
rapiers are afraid of goose-quills and dare
scarce come thither.

HAMLET

What, are they children? Who maintains 'em?
How are they escoted? Will they pursue the
quality no longer than they can sing? Will

they not say afterwards, if they should grow
themselves to common players—as it is most
like, if their means are no better—their writers
do them wrong, to make them exclaim against
their own succession?

ROSENCRANTZ

Faith, there has been much to do on both
sides; and the nation holds it no sin to tarre
them to controversy: there was, for a while, no
money bid for argument, unless the poet and
the player went to cuffs in the question.

HAMLET

Is't possible?

GUILDENSTERN

O, there has been much throwing about of
brains.

HAMLET

Do the boys carry it away?

ROSENCRANTZ

Ay, that they do, my lord; Hercules and his
load too.

HAMLET

It is not very strange; for mine uncle is king of
Denmark, and those that would make mows at
him while my father lived, give twenty, forty,
fifty, an hundred ducats a-piece for his picture
in little. 'Sblood, there is something in this

more than natural, if philosophy could find it out.

Flourish of trumpets within

GUILDENSTERN

There are the players.

HAMLET

Gentlemen, you are welcome to Elsinore. Your hands, come then: the appurtenance of welcome is fashion and ceremony: let me comply with you in this garb, lest my extent to the players, which, I tell you, must show fairly outward, should more appear like entertainment than yours. You are welcome: but my uncle-father and aunt-mother are deceived.

GUILDENSTERN

In what, my dear lord?

HAMLET

I am but mad north-north-west: when the wind is southerly I know a hawk from a handsaw.

Enter POLONIUS

LORD POLONIUS

Well be with you, gentlemen!

HAMLET

Hark you, Guildenstern; and you too: at each ear a hearer: that great baby you see there is not yet out of his swaddling-clouts.

ROSENCRANTZ

Happily he's the second time come to them; for they say an old man is twice a child.

HAMLET

I will prophesy he comes to tell me of the players; mark it. You say right, sir: o' Monday morning; 'twas so indeed.

LORD POLONIUS

My lord, I have news to tell you.

HAMLET

My lord, I have news to tell you.

When Roscius was an actor in Rome——

LORD POLONIUS

The actors are come hither, my lord.

HAMLET

Buz, buz!

LORD POLONIUS

Upon mine honour——

HAMLET

Then came each actor on his ass——

LORD POLONIUS

The best actors in the world, either for tragedy, comedy, history, pastoral, pastoral-comical, historical-pastoral, tragical-historical, tragical-comical-historical-pastoral, scene individable, or poem unlimited: Seneca cannot be too heavy, nor Plautus too light. For the law of writ and the liberty, these are the only men.

HAMLET

O Jephthah, judge of Israel, what a treasure hadst thou!

LORD POLONIUS

What a treasure had he, my lord?

HAMLET

Why,

'One fair daughter and no more,

The which he loved passing well.'

LORD POLONIUS

(Aside) Still on my daughter.

HAMLET

Am I not i' the right, old Jephthah?

LORD POLONIUS

If you call me Jephthah, my lord, I have a daughter that I love passing well.

HAMLET

Nay, that follows not.

LORD POLONIUS

What follows, then, my lord?

HAMLET

Why, 'As by lot, God wot,' and then, you know, 'It came to pass, as most like it was,'—the first row of the pious chanson will show you more; for look, where my abridgement comes.

You are welcome, masters; welcome, all. I am glad to see thee well. Welcome, good friends. O, my old friend! thy face is valenced since I saw thee last: comest thou to beard me in Denmark? What, my young lady and mistress! By'r lady, your ladyship is nearer to heaven than when I saw you last, by the altitude of a chopine. Pray God, your voice, like apiece of uncurrent gold, be not cracked within the ring. Masters, you are all welcome. We'll e'en to't like French falconers, fly at any thing we see: we'll have a speech straight: come, give us a taste of your quality; come, a passionate speech.

FIRST PLAYER

What speech, my lord?

HAMLET

I heard thee speak me a speech once, but it was never acted; or, if it was, not above once; for the play, I remember, pleased not the million; 'twas caviare to the general: but it was—as I received it, and others, whose judgments in such matters cried in the top of mine—an excellent play, well digested in the scenes, set down with as much modesty as cunning. I remember, one said there were no sallets in the lines to make the matter savoury, nor no matter in the phrase that might indict the author of affectation; but called it an honest method, as wholesome as sweet, and by very much more handsome than fine. One speech in it I chiefly loved: 'twas Aeneas' tale to Dido; and thereabout of it especially, where he speaks of Priam's slaughter: if it live in your memory, begin at this line: let me see, let me see—'The rugged Pyrrhus, like the Hyrcanian beast,'— it is not so:—it begins with Pyrrhus:—'The rugged Pyrrhus, he whose sable arms, Black as his purpose, did the night resemble When he lay couched in the ominous horse, Hath now this dread and black complexion smear'd With heraldry more dismal; head to foot Now is he total gules; horridly trick'd With blood of fathers, mothers, daughters, sons, Baked and impasted with the parching streets, That lend a tyrannous and damned light To their lord's murder: roasted in wrath and fire, And thus o'er-sized with coagulate gore, With eyes like carbuncles, the hellish Pyrrhus Old grandsire Priam seeks.' So, proceed you.

LORD POLONIUS

Fore God, my lord, well spoken, with good accent and good discretion.

FIRST PLAYER
    'Anon he finds him
    Striking too short at Greeks; his antique sword,
    Rebellious to his arm, lies where it falls,
    Repugnant to command: unequal match'd,
    Pyrrhus at Priam drives; in rage strikes wide;
    But with the whiff and wind of his fell sword
    The unnerved father falls. Then senseless Ilium,
    Seeming to feel this blow, with flaming top
    Stoops to his base, and with a hideous crash
    Takes prisoner Pyrrhus' ear: for, lo! his sword,
    Which was declining on the milky head
    Of reverend Priam, seem'd i' the air to stick:
    So, as a painted tyrant, Pyrrhus stood,
    And like a neutral to his will and matter,
    Did nothing.
    But, as we often see, against some storm,
    A silence in the heavens, the rack stand still,
    The bold winds speechless and the orb below
    As hush as death, anon the dreadful thunder
    Doth rend the region, so, after Pyrrhus' pause,
    Aroused vengeance sets him new a-work;
    And never did the Cyclops' hammers fall
    On Mars's armour forged for proof eterne
    With less remorse than Pyrrhus' bleeding sword
    Now falls on Priam.
    Out, out, thou strumpet, Fortune! All you gods,

In general synod take away her power;
Break all the spokes and fellies from her wheel,
And bowl the round nave down the hill of
    heaven,
As low as to the fiends!'
LORD POLONIUS
    This is too long.
HAMLET
    It shall to the barber's, with your beard. Prithee,
    say on: he's for a jig or a tale of bawdry, or he
    sleeps: say on: come to Hecuba.
FIRST PLAYER
    'But who, O, who had seen the mobled
    queen—'
HAMLET
    'The mobled queen?'
LORD POLONIUS
    That's good; 'mobled queen' is good.
FIRST PLAYER
    'Run barefoot up and down, threatening the
        flames
    With bisson rheum; a clout upon that head
    Where late the diadem stood, and for a robe,
    About her lank and all o'er-teemed loins,
    A blanket, in the alarm of fear caught up;
    Who this had seen, with tongue in venom
        steep'd,

'Gainst Fortune's state would treason have
    pronounced:
But if the gods themselves did see her then
When she saw Pyrrhus make malicious sport
In mincing with his sword her husband's limbs,
The instant burst of clamour that she made,
Unless things mortal move them not at all,
Would have made milch the burning eyes of
    heaven,
And passion in the gods.'

LORD POLONIUS

Look, whether he has not turned his colour
and has tears in's eyes. Pray you, no more.

HAMLET

'Tis well: I'll have thee speak out the rest soon.
Good my lord, will you see the players well
bestowed? Do you hear, let them be well used;
for they are the abstract and brief chronicles
of the time: after your death you were better
have a bad epitaph than their ill report while
you live.

LORD POLONIUS

My lord, I will use them according to their
desert.

HAMLET

God's bodykins, man, much better: use every
man after his desert, and who should 'scape

whipping? Use them after your own honour and dignity: the less they deserve, the more merit is in your bounty. Take them in.

LORD POLONIUS

Come, sirs.

HAMLET

Follow him, friends: we'll hear a play to-morrow.

Exit POLONIUS with all the Players but the First

Dost thou hear me, old friend; can you play the Murder of Gonzago?

FIRST PLAYER

Ay, my lord.

HAMLET

We'll ha't to-morrow night. You could, for a need, study a speech of some dozen or sixteen lines, which I would set down and insert in't, could you not?

FIRST PLAYER

Ay, my lord.

HAMLET

Very well. Follow that lord; and look you mock him not.

Exit First Player

My good friends, I'll leave you till night: you
are welcome to Elsinore.
ROSENCRANTZ
Good, my lord!
HAMLET
Ay, so, God be wi' ye;

> *Exeunt ROSENCRANTZ and*
> *GUILDENSTERN*

Now I am alone.
O, what a rogue and peasant slave am I!
Is it not monstrous that this player here,
But in a fiction, in a dream of passion,
Could force his soul so to his own conceit
That from her working all his visage wann'd,
Tears in his eyes, distraction in's aspect,
A broken voice, and his whole function suiting
With forms to his conceit? and all for nothing!
For Hecuba!
What's Hecuba to him, or he to Hecuba,
That he should weep for her? What would
    he do,
Had he the motive and the cue for passion
That I have? He would drown the stage with
    tears
And cleave the general ear with horrid speech,
Make mad the guilty and appal the free,

Confound the ignorant, and amaze indeed
The very faculties of eyes and ears. Yet I,
A dull and muddy-mettled rascal, peak,
Like John-a-dreams, unpregnant of my cause,
And can say nothing; no, not for a king,
Upon whose property and most dear life
A damn'd defeat was made. Am I a coward?
Who calls me villain? breaks my pate across?
Plucks off my beard, and blows it in my face?
Tweaks me by the nose? gives me the lie i' the
    throat,
As deep as to the lungs? who does me this?
Ha!
'Swounds, I should take it: for it cannot be
But I am pigeon-liver'd and lack gall
To make oppression bitter, or ere this
I should have fatted all the region kites
With this slave's offal: bloody, bawdy villain!
Remorseless, treacherous, lecherous, kindless
    villain!
O, vengeance!
Why, what an ass am I! This is most brave,
That I, the son of a dear father murder'd,
Prompted to my revenge by heaven and hell,
Must, like a whore, unpack my heart with words,
And fall a-cursing, like a very drab,
A scullion!

Fie upon't! foh! About, my brain! I have heard
That guilty creatures sitting at a play
Have by the very cunning of the scene
Been struck so to the soul that presently
They have proclaim'd their malefactions;
For murder, though it have no tongue, will
    speak
With most miraculous organ. I'll have these
    players
Play something like the murder of my father
Before mine uncle: I'll observe his looks;
I'll tent him to the quick: if he but blench,
I know my course. The spirit that I have seen
May be the devil: and the devil hath power
To assume a pleasing shape; yea, and perhaps
Out of my weakness and my melancholy,
As he is very potent with such spirits,
Abuses me to damn me: I'll have grounds
More relative than this: the play 's the thing
Wherein I'll catch the conscience of the king.

Exit

Act 3

SCENE I.
A ROOM IN THE CASTLE.

Enter KING CLAUDIUS, QUEEN GERTRUDE,
POLONIUS, OPHELIA, ROSENCRANTZ, and
GUILDENSTERN

KING CLAUDIUS

    And can you, by no drift of circumstance,

    Get from him why he puts on this confusion,

    Grating so harshly all his days of quiet

    With turbulent and dangerous lunacy?

ROSENCRANTZ

    He does confess he feels himself distracted;

    But from what cause he will by no means speak.

GUILDENSTERN

    Nor do we find him forward to be sounded,

    But, with a crafty madness, keeps aloof,

When we would bring him on to some confession
Of his true state.
QUEEN GERTRUDE
Did he receive you well?
ROSENCRANTZ
Most like a gentleman.
GUILDENSTERN
But with much forcing of his disposition.
ROSENCRANTZ
Niggard of question; but, of our demands,
Most free in his reply.
QUEEN GERTRUDE
Did you assay him?
To any pastime?
ROSENCRANTZ
Madam, it so fell out, that certain players
We o'er-raught on the way: of these we told him;
And there did seem in him a kind of joy
To hear of it: they are about the court,
And, as I think, they have already order
This night to play before him.
LORD POLONIUS
'Tis most true:
And he beseech'd me to entreat your majesties
To hear and see the matter.

KING CLAUDIUS

With all my heart; and it doth much content me
To hear him so inclined.
Good gentlemen, give him a further edge,
And drive his purpose on to these delights.

ROSENCRANTZ

We shall, my lord.

Exeunt ROSENCRANTZ and
GUILDENSTERN

KING CLAUDIUS

Sweet Gertrude, leave us too;
For we have closely sent for Hamlet hither,
That he, as 'twere by accident, may here
Affront Ophelia:
Her father and myself, lawful espials,
Will so bestow ourselves that, seeing, unseen,
We may of their encounter frankly judge,
And gather by him, as he is behaved,
If 't be the affliction of his love or no
That thus he suffers for.

QUEEN GERTRUDE

I shall obey you.
And for your part, Ophelia, I do wish
That your good beauties be the happy cause
Of Hamlet's wildness: so shall I hope your
virtues

Will bring him to his wonted way again,
To both your honours.

OPHELIA
Madam, I wish it may.

Exit QUEEN GERTRUDE

LORD POLONIUS
Ophelia, walk you here. Gracious, so please you,
We will bestow ourselves.

To OPHELIA

Read on this book;
That show of such an exercise may colour
Your loneliness. We are oft to blame in this—
'Tis too much proved—that with devotion's
    visage
And pious action we do sugar o'er
The devil himself.

KING CLAUDIUS
(Aside) O, 'tis too true!
How smart a lash that speech doth give my
    conscience!
The harlot's cheek, beautied with plastering art,
Is not more ugly to the thing that helps it
Than is my deed to my most painted word:
O heavy burthen!

LORD POLONIUS

I hear him coming: let's withdraw, my lord.

Exeunt KING CLAUDIUS and POLONIUS

Enter HAMLET

HAMLET

To be, or not to be: that is the question:

Whether 'tis nobler in the mind to suffer

The slings and arrows of outrageous fortune,

Or to take arms against a sea of troubles,

And by opposing end them? To die: to sleep;

No more; and by a sleep to say we end

The heart-ache and the thousand natural shocks

That flesh is heir to, 'tis a consummation

Devoutly to be wish'd. To die, to sleep;

To sleep: perchance to dream: ay, there's the rub;

For in that sleep of death what dreams may come

When we have shuffled off this mortal coil,

Must give us pause: there's the respect

That makes calamity of so long life;

For who would bear the whips and scorns of time,

The oppressor's wrong, the proud man's contumely,

The pangs of despised love, the law's delay,

The insolence of office and the spurns
That patient merit of the unworthy takes,
When he himself might his quietus make
With a bare bodkin? who would fardels bear,
To grunt and sweat under a weary life,
But that the dread of something after death,
The undiscover'd country from whose bourn
No traveller returns, puzzles the will
And makes us rather bear those ills we have
Than fly to others that we know not of?
Thus conscience does make cowards of us all;
And thus the native hue of resolution
Is sicklied o'er with the pale cast of thought,
And enterprises of great pith and moment
With this regard their currents turn awry,
And lose the name of action. Soft you now!
The fair Ophelia! Nymph, in thy orisons
Be all my sins remember'd.

OPHELIA

Good my lord,
How does your honour for this many a day?

HAMLET

I humbly thank you; well, well, well.

OPHELIA

My lord, I have remembrances of yours,
That I have longed long to re-deliver;
I pray you, now receive them.

HAMLET

No, not I;

I never gave you aught.

OPHELIA

My honour'd lord, you know right well you did;

And, with them, words of so sweet breath composed

As made the things more rich: their perfume lost,

Take these again; for to the noble mind

Rich gifts wax poor when givers prove unkind.

There, my lord.

HAMLET

Ha, ha! are you honest?

OPHELIA

My lord?

HAMLET

Are you fair?

OPHELIA

What means your lordship?

HAMLET

That if you be honest and fair, your honesty should admit no discourse to your beauty.

OPHELIA

Could beauty, my lord, have better commerce than with honesty?

HAMLET

Ay, truly; for the power of beauty will sooner transform honesty from what it is to a bawd than the force of honesty can translate beauty into his likeness: this was sometime a paradox, but now the time gives it proof. I did love you once.

OPHELIA

Indeed, my lord, you made me believe so.

HAMLET

You should not have believed me; for virtue cannot so inoculate our old stock but we shall relish of it: I loved you not.

OPHELIA

I was the more deceived.

HAMLET

Get thee to a nunnery: why wouldst thou be a breeder of sinners? I am myself indifferent honest; but yet I could accuse me of such things that it were better my mother had not borne me: I am very proud, revengeful, ambitious, with more offences at my beck than I have thoughts to put them in, imagination to give them shape, or time to act them in. What should such fellows as I do crawling between earth and heaven? We are arrant knaves, all; believe none of us. Go thy ways to a nunnery. Where's your father?

OPHELIA

At home, my lord.

HAMLET

Let the doors be shut upon him, that he may play the fool no where but in's own house. Farewell.

OPHELIA

O, help him, you sweet heavens!

HAMLET

If thou dost marry, I'll give thee this plague for thy dowry: be thou as chaste as ice, as pure as snow, thou shalt not escape calumny. Get thee to a nunnery, go: farewell. Or, if thou wilt needs marry, marry a fool; for wise men know well enough what monsters you make of them. To a nunnery, go, and quickly too. Farewell.

OPHELIA

O heavenly powers, restore him!

HAMLET

I have heard of your paintings too, well enough; God has given you one face, and you make yourselves another: you jig, you amble, and you lisp, and nick name God's creatures, and make your wantonness your ignorance. Go to, I'll no more on't; it hath made me mad. I say, we will have no more marriages: those that are

married already, all but one, shall live; the rest
shall keep as they are. To a nunnery, go.

Exit

OPHELIA
O, what a noble mind is here o'erthrown!
The courtier's, soldier's, scholar's, eye, tongue,
sword;
The expectancy and rose of the fair state,
The glass of fashion and the mould of form,
The observed of all observers, quite, quite
down!
And I, of ladies most deject and wretched,
That suck'd the honey of his music vows,
Now see that noble and most sovereign reason,
Like sweet bells jangled, out of tune and harsh;
That unmatch'd form and feature of blown
youth
Blasted with ecstasy: O, woe is me,
To have seen what I have seen, see what I see!

Re-enter KING CLAUDIUS and POLONIUS
KING CLAUDIUS
Love! his affections do not that way tend;
Nor what he spake, though it lack'd form a
little,

Was not like madness. There's something in
    his soul,
O'er which his melancholy sits on brood;
And I do doubt the hatch and the disclose
Will be some danger: which for to prevent,
I have in quick determination
Thus set it down: he shall with speed to England,
For the demand of our neglected tribute
Haply the seas and countries different
With variable objects shall expel
This something-settled matter in his heart,
hereon his brains still beating puts him thus
From fashion of himself. What think you on't?

LORD POLONIUS

It shall do well: but yet do I believe
The origin and commencement of his grief
Sprung from neglected love. How now, Ophelia!
You need not tell us what Lord Hamlet said;
We heard it all. My lord, do as you please;
But, if you hold it fit, after the play
Let his queen mother all alone entreat him
To show his grief: let her be round with him;
And I'll be placed, so please you, in the ear
Of all their conference. If she find him not,
To England send him, or confine him where
Your wisdom best shall think.

KING CLAUDIUS

It shall be so:

Madness in great ones must not unwatch'd go.

Exeunt

SCENE II. A HALL IN THE CASTLE.

Enter HAMLET and Players

HAMLET

Speak the speech, I pray you, as I pronounced it to you, trippingly on the tongue: but if you mouth it, as many of your players do, I had as lief the town-crier spoke my lines. Nor do not saw the air too much with your hand, thus, but use all gently; for in the very torrent, tempest, and, as I may say, the whirlwind of passion, you must acquire and beget a temperance that may give it smoothness. O, it offends me to the soul to hear a robustious periwig-pated fellow tear a passion to tatters, to very rags, to split the ears of the groundlings, who for the most part are capable of nothing but inexplicable dumbshows and noise: I would have such a fellow whipped for o'erdoing Termagant; it out-herods Herod: pray you, avoid it.

FIRST PLAYER

I warrant your honour.

HAMLET

Be not too tame neither, but let your own discretion be your tutor: suit the action to the word, the word to the action; with this special o'erstep not the modesty of nature: for any thing so overdone is from the purpose of playing, whose end, both at the first and now, was and is, to hold, as 'twere, the mirror up to nature; to show virtue her own feature, scorn her own image, and the very age and body of the time his form and pressure. Now this overdone, or come tardy off, though it make the unskilful laugh, cannot but make the judicious grieve; the censure of the which one must in your allowance o'erweigh a whole theatre of others. O, there be players that I have seen play, and heard others praise, and that highly, not to speak it profanely, that, neither having the accent of Christians nor the gait of Christian, pagan, nor man, have so strutted and bellowed that I have thought some of nature's journeymen had made men and not made them well, they imitated humanity so abominably.

FIRST PLAYER

I hope we have reformed that indifferently with us, sir.

HAMLET

O, reform it altogether. And let those that
play your clowns speak no more than is set
down for them; for there be of them that will
themselves laugh, to set on some quantity of
barren spectators to laugh too; though, in the
mean time, some necessary question of the play
be then to be considered: that's villanous, and
shows a most pitiful ambition in the fool that
uses it. Go, make you ready.

Exeunt Players

*Enter POLONIUS, ROSENCRANTZ, and
GUILDENSTERN*

How now, my lord! I will the king hear this
piece of work?
LORD POLONIUS

And the queen too, and that presently.
HAMLET

Bid the players make haste.

Exit POLONIUS

Will you two help to hasten them?
ROSENCRANTZ AND GUILDENSTERN

We will, my lord.

*Exeunt ROSENCRANTZ and
GUILDENSTERN*

HAMLET

What ho! Horatio!

Enter HORATIO

HORATIO

Here, sweet lord, at your service.

HAMLET

Horatio, thou art e'en as just a man

As e'er my conversation coped withal.

HORATIO

O, my dear lord—

HAMLET

Nay, do not think I flatter;

For what advancement may I hope from thee

That no revenue hast but thy good spirits,

To feed and clothe thee? Why should the poor

be flatter'd?

No, let the candied tongue lick absurd pomp,

And crook the pregnant hinges of the knee

Where thrift may follow fawning. Dost thou

hear?

Since my dear soul was mistress of her choice

And could of men distinguish, her election

Hath seal'd thee for herself; for thou hast been

As one, in suffering all, that suffers nothing,

A man that fortune's buffets and rewards

Hast ta'en with equal thanks: and blest are those
Whose blood and judgment are so well
    commingled,
That they are not a pipe for fortune's finger
To sound what stop she please. Give me that
    man
That is not passion's slave, and I will wear him
In my heart's core, ay, in my heart of heart,
As I do thee. Something too much of this.
There is a play to-night before the king;
One scene of it comes near the circumstance
Which I have told thee of my father's death:
I prithee, when thou seest that act afoot,
Even with the very comment of thy soul
Observe mine uncle: if his occulted guilt
Do not itself unkennel in one speech,
It is a damned ghost that we have seen,
And my imaginations are as foul
As Vulcan's stithy. Give him heedful note;
For I mine eyes will rivet to his face,
And after we will both our judgments join
In censure of his seeming.

HORATIO

Well, my lord:
If he steal aught the whilst this play is playing,
And 'scape detecting, I will pay the theft.

HAMLET

They are coming to the play; I must be idle:
Get you a place.

Danish march. A flourish. Enter KING CLAUDIUS, QUEEN GERTRUDE, POLONIUS, OPHELIA, ROSENCRANTZ, GUILDENSTERN, and others

KING CLAUDIUS

How fares our cousin Hamlet?

HAMLET

Excellent, i' faith; of the chameleon's dish: I eat the air, promise-crammed: you cannot feed capons so.

KING CLAUDIUS

I have nothing with this answer, Hamlet; these words are not mine.

HAMLET

No, nor mine now.

To POLONIUS

My lord, you played once i' the university, you say?

LORD POLONIUS

That did I, my lord; and was accounted a good actor.

HAMLET

What did you enact?

LORD POLONIUS

I did enact Julius Caesar: I was killed i' the
Capitol; Brutus killed me.

HAMLET

It was a brute part of him to kill so capital a
calf there. Be the players ready?

ROSENCRANTZ

Ay, my lord; they stay upon your patience.

QUEEN GERTRUDE

Come hither, my dear Hamlet, sit by me.

HAMLET

No, good mother, here's metal more attractive.

LORD POLONIUS

(To KING CLAUDIUS) O, ho! do you mark
that?

HAMLET

Lady, shall I lie in your lap?

Lying down at OPHELIA's feet

OPHELIA

No, my lord.

HAMLET

I mean, my head upon your lap?

OPHELIA

Ay, my lord.

HAMLET

Do you think I meant country matters?

OPHELIA

I think nothing, my lord.

HAMLET

That's a fair thought to lie between maids' legs.

OPHELIA

What is, my lord?

HAMLET

Nothing.

OPHELIA

You are merry, my lord.

HAMLET

Who, I?

OPHELIA

Ay, my lord.

HAMLET

O God, your only jig-maker. What should a man do but be merry? for, look you, how cheerfully my mother looks, and my father died within these two hours.

OPHELIA

Nay, 'tis twice two months, my lord.

HAMLET

So long? Nay then, let the devil wear black, for

I'll have a suit of sables. O heavens! die two months ago, and not forgotten yet? Then there's hope a great man's memory may outlive his life half a year: but, by'r lady, he must build churches, then; or else shall he suffer not thinking on, with the hobby-horse, whose epitaph is 'For, O, for, O, the hobby-horse is forgot.'

Hautboys play. The dumb-show enters Enter a King and a Queen very lovingly; the Queen embracing him, and he her. She kneels, and makes show of protestation unto him. He takes her up, and declines his head upon her neck: lays him down upon a bank of flowers: she, seeing him asleep, leaves him. Anon comes in a fellow, takes off his crown, kisses it, and pours poison in the King's ears, and exit. The Queen returns; finds the King dead, and makes passionate action. The Poisoner, with some two or three Mutes, comes in again, seeming to lament with her. The dead body is carried away. The Poisoner wooes the Queen with gifts: she seems loath and unwilling awhile, but in the end accepts his love

Exeunt

OPHELIA

What means this, my lord?

HAMLET

Marry, this is miching mallecho; it means mischief.

OPHELIA

Belike this show imports the argument of the
play.

Enter Prologue

HAMLET

We shall know by this fellow: the players
cannot keep counsel; they'll tell all.

OPHELIA

Will he tell us what this show meant?

HAMLET

Ay, or any show that you'll show him: be not
you ashamed to show, he'll not shame to tell
you what it means.

OPHELIA

You are naught, you are naught: I'll mark the
play.

PROLOGUE

For us, and for our tragedy,
Here stooping to your clemency,
We beg your hearing patiently.

Exit

HAMLET

Is this a prologue, or the posy of a ring?

OPHELIA

'Tis brief, my lord.

HAMLET

As woman's love.

Enter two Players, King and Queen

PLAYER KING

Full thirty times hath Phoebus' cart gone round
Neptune's salt wash and Tellus' orbed ground,
And thirty dozen moons with borrow'd sheen
About the world have times twelve thirties
    been,
Since love our hearts and Hymen did our hands
Unite commutual in most sacred bands.

PLAYER QUEEN

So many journeys may the sun and moon
Make us again count o'er ere love be done!
But, woe is me, you are so sick of late,
So far from cheer and from your former state,
That I distrust you. Yet, though I distrust,
Discomfort you, my lord, it nothing must:
For women's fear and love holds quantity;
In neither aught, or in extremity.
Now, what my love is, proof hath made you
    know;
And as my love is sized, my fear is so:
Where love is great, the littlest doubts are fear;
Where little fears grow great, great love grows
    there.

PLAYER KING

'Faith, I must leave thee, love, and shortly too;
My operant powers their functions leave to do:
And thou shalt live in this fair world behind,
Honour'd, beloved; and haply one as kind
For husband shalt thou—

PLAYER QUEEN

O, confound the rest!
Such love must needs be treason in my breast:
In second husband let me be accurst!
None wed the second but who kill'd the first.

HAMLET

(Aside) Wormwood, wormwood.

PLAYER QUEEN

The instances that second marriage move
Are base respects of thrift, but none of love:
A second time I kill my husband dead,
When second husband kisses me in bed.

PLAYER KING

I do believe you think what now you speak;
But what we do determine oft we break.
Purpose is but the slave to memory,
Of violent birth, but poor validity;
Which now, like fruit unripe, sticks on the tree;
But fall, unshaken, when they mellow be.
Most necessary 'tis that we forget
To pay ourselves what to ourselves is debt:

What to ourselves in passion we propose,
The passion ending, doth the purpose lose.
The violence of either grief or joy
Their own enactures with themselves destroy:
Where joy most revels, grief doth most lament;
Grief joys, joy grieves, on slender accident.
This world is not for aye, nor 'tis not strange
That even our loves should with our fortunes
    change;
For 'tis a question left us yet to prove,
Whether love lead fortune, or else fortune love.
The great man down, you mark his favourite flies;
The poor advanced makes friends of enemies.
And hitherto doth love on fortune tend;
For who not needs shall never lack a friend,
And who in want a hollow friend doth try,
Directly seasons him his enemy.
But, orderly to end where I begun,
Our wills and fates do so contrary run
That our devices still are overthrown;
Our thoughts are ours, their ends none of our
    own:
So think thou wilt no second husband wed;
But die thy thoughts when thy first lord is dead.

PLAYER QUEEN

Nor earth to me give food, nor heaven light!
Sport and repose lock from me day and night!

To desperation turn my trust and hope!
An anchor's cheer in prison be my scope!
Each opposite that blanks the face of joy
Meet what I would have well and it destroy!
Both here and hence pursue me lasting strife,
If, once a widow, ever I be wife!

HAMLET

If she should break it now!

PLAYER KING

'Tis deeply sworn. Sweet, leave me here awhile;
My spirits grow dull, and fain I would beguile
The tedious day with sleep.

Sleeps

PLAYER QUEEN

Sleep rock thy brain,
And never come mischance between us twain!

Exit

HAMLET

Madam, how like you this play?

QUEEN GERTRUDE

The lady protests too much, methinks.

HAMLET

O, but she'll keep her word.

KING CLAUDIUS

Have you heard the argument? Is there no
offence in 't?

HAMLET

No, no, they do but jest, poison in jest; no
offence i' the world.

KING CLAUDIUS

What do you call the play?

HAMLET

The Mouse-trap. Marry, how? Tropically. This
play is the image of a murder done in Vienna:
Gonzago is the duke's name; his wife, Baptista:
you shall see anon; 'tis a knavish piece of work:
but what o' that? your majesty and we that have
free souls, it touches us not: let the galled jade
wince, our withers are unwrung.

Enter LUCIANUS

This is one Lucianus, nephew to the king.

OPHELIA

You are as good as a chorus, my lord.

HAMLET

I could interpret between you and your love, if
I could see the puppets dallying.

OPHELIA

You are keen, my lord, you are keen.

HAMLET

It would cost you a groaning to take off my
edge.

OPHELIA

Still better, and worse.

HAMLET

So you must take your husbands. Begin, murderer; pox, leave thy damnable faces, and begin. Come: 'the croaking raven doth bellow for revenge.'

LUCIANUS

Thoughts black, hands apt, drugs fit, and time
    agreeing;
Confederate season, else no creature seeing;
Thou mixture rank, of midnight weeds
    collected,
With Hecate's ban thrice blasted, thrice infected,
Thy natural magic and dire property,
On wholesome life usurp immediately.

Pours the poison into the sleeper's ears

HAMLET

He poisons him i' the garden for's estate. His name's Gonzago: the story is extant, and writ in choice Italian: you shall see anon how the murderer gets the love of Gonzago's wife.

OPHELIA

The king rises.

HAMLET

What, frighted with false fire!

QUEEN GERTRUDE

How fares my lord?

LORD POLONIUS

Give o'er the play.

KING CLAUDIUS

Give me some light: away!

ALL

Lights, lights, lights!

Exeunt all but HAMLET and
HORATIO

HAMLET

Why, let the stricken deer go weep,

The hart ungalled play;

For some must watch, while some must sleep:

So runs the world away.

Would not this, sir, and a forest of feathers—
     if the rest of my fortunes turn Turk with
     me—with two

Provincial roses on my razed shoes, get me a
     fellowship in a cry of players, sir?

HORATIO

Half a share.

HAMLET

A whole one, I.

For thou dost know, O Damon dear,

This realm dismantled was

Of Jove himself; and now reigns here
A very, very—pajock.

HORATIO
You might have rhymed.

HAMLET
O good Horatio, I'll take the ghost's word for a
thousand pound. Didst perceive?

HORATIO
Very well, my lord.

HAMLET
Upon the talk of the poisoning?

HORATIO
I did very well note him.

HAMLET
Ah, ha! Come, some music! come, the recorders!
For if the king like not the comedy,
Why then, belike, he likes it not, perdy.
Come, some music!

Re-enter ROSENCRANTZ and GUILDENSTERN

GUILDENSTERN
Good my lord, vouchsafe me a word with you.

HAMLET
Sir, a whole history.

GUILDENSTERN
The king, sir—

HAMLET

Ay, sir, what of him?

GUILDENSTERN

Is in his retirement marvellous distempered.

HAMLET

With drink, sir?

GUILDENSTERN

No, my lord, rather with choler.

HAMLET

Your wisdom should show itself more richer to signify this to his doctor; for, for me to put him to his purgation would perhaps plunge him into far more choler.

GUILDENSTERN

Good my lord, put your discourse into some frame and start not so wildly from my affair.

HAMLET

I am tame, sir: pronounce.

GUILDENSTERN

The queen, your mother, in most great affliction of spirit, hath sent me to you.

HAMLET

You are welcome.

GUILDENSTERN

Nay, good my lord, this courtesy is not of the right breed. If it shall please you to make me a wholesome answer, I will do your mother's commandment: if not, your pardon and my return shall be the end of my business.

HAMLET

Sir, I cannot.

GUILDENSTERN

What, my lord?

HAMLET

Make you a wholesome answer; my wit's diseased: but, sir, such answer as I can make, you shall command; or, rather, as you say, my mother: therefore no more, but to the matter: my mother, you say—

ROSENCRANTZ

Then thus she says; your behavior hath struck her into amazement and admiration.

HAMLET

O wonderful son, that can so astonish a mother! But is there no sequel at the heels of this mother's admiration? Impart.

ROSENCRANTZ

She desires to speak with you in her closet, ere you go to bed.

HAMLET

We shall obey, were she ten times our mother. Have you any further trade with us?

ROSENCRANTZ

My lord, you once did love me.

HAMLET

So I do still, by these pickers and stealers.

ROSENCRANTZ

Good my lord, what is your cause of distemper?
you do, surely, bar the door upon your own
liberty, if you deny your griefs to your friend.

HAMLET

Sir, I lack advancement.

ROSENCRANTZ

How can that be, when you have the voice
of the king himself for your succession in
Denmark?

HAMLET

Ay, but sir, 'While the grass grows,'—the
proverb is something musty.

Re-enter Players with recorders

O, the recorders! let me see one. To withdraw
with you: why do you go about to recover the
wind of me, as if you would drive me into a
toil?

GUILDENSTERN

O, my lord, if my duty be too bold, my love is
too unmannerly.

HAMLET

I do not well understand that. Will you play
upon this pipe?

GUILDENSTERN

My lord, I cannot.

HAMLET

I pray you.

GUILDENSTERN

Believe me, I cannot.

HAMLET

I do beseech you.

GUILDENSTERN

I know no touch of it, my lord.

HAMLET

'Tis as easy as lying: govern these ventages with your lingers and thumb, give it breath with your mouth, and it will discourse most eloquent music. Look you, these are the stops.

GUILDENSTERN

But these cannot I command to any utterance of harmony; I have not the skill.

HAMLET

Why, look you now, how unworthy a thing you make of me! You would play upon me; you would seem to know my stops; you would pluck out the heart of my mystery; you would sound me from my lowest note to the top of my compass: and there is much music, excellent voice, in this little organ; yet cannot you make it speak. 'Sblood, do you think I am easier to be played on than a pipe? Call me what instrument you will, though you can fret me, yet you cannot play upon me.

Enter POLONIUS

God bless you, sir!

LORD POLONIUS

My lord, the queen would speak with you, and presently.

HAMLET

Do you see yonder cloud that's almost in shape of a camel?

LORD POLONIUS

By the mass, and 'tis like a camel, indeed.

HAMLET

Methinks it is like a weasel.

LORD POLONIUS

It is backed like a weasel.

HAMLET

Or like a whale?

LORD POLONIUS

Very like a whale.

HAMLET

Then I will come to my mother by and by. They fool me to the top of my bent. I will come by and by.

LORD POLONIUS

I will say so.

HAMLET

By and by is easily said.

Exit POLONIUS

Leave me, friends.

Exeunt all but HAMLET

'Tis now the very witching time of night,
When churchyards yawn and hell itself breathes
out
Contagion to this world: now could I drink
hot blood,
And do such bitter business as the day
Would quake to look on. Soft! now to my
mother.
O heart, lose not thy nature; let not ever
The soul of Nero enter this firm bosom:
Let me be cruel, not unnatural:
I will speak daggers to her, but use none;
My tongue and soul in this be hypocrites;
How in my words soever she be shent,
To give them seals never, my soul, consent!

Exit

SCENE III. A ROOM IN THE CASTLE.

Enter KING CLAUDIUS, ROSENCRANTZ, and GUILDENSTERN

KING CLAUDIUS

 I like him not, nor stands it safe with us
 To let his madness range. Therefore prepare
  you;
 I your commission will forthwith dispatch,
 And he to England shall along with you:
 The terms of our estate may not endure
 Hazard so dangerous as doth hourly grow
 Out of his lunacies.

GUILDENSTERN

 We will ourselves provide:
 Most holy and religious fear it is
 To keep those many many bodies safe
 That live and feed upon your majesty.

ROSENCRANTZ

 The single and peculiar life is bound,
 With all the strength and armour of the mind,
 To keep itself from noyance; but much more
 That spirit upon whose weal depend and rest
 The lives of many. The cease of majesty
 Dies not alone; but, like a gulf, doth draw
 What's near it with it: it is a massy wheel,
 Fix'd on the summit of the highest mount,

To whose huge spokes ten thousand lesser
    things
Are mortised and adjoin'd; which, when it falls,
Each small annexment, petty consequence,
Attends the boisterous ruin. Never alone
Did the king sigh, but with a general groan.

KING CLAUDIUS

Arm you, I pray you, to this speedy voyage;
For we will fetters put upon this fear,
Which now goes too free-footed.

ROSENCRANTZ AND GUILDENSTERN

We will haste us.

        Exeunt ROSENCRANTZ and
        GUILDENSTERN

Enter POLONIUS

LORD POLONIUS

My lord, he's going to his mother's closet:
Behind the arras I'll convey myself,
To hear the process; and warrant she'll tax him
    home:
And, as you said, and wisely was it said,
'Tis meet that some more audience than a
    mother,
Since nature makes them partial, should
    o'erhear
The speech, of vantage. Fare you well, my liege:

I'll call upon you ere you go to bed,
And tell you what I know.
KING CLAUDIUS
    Thanks, dear my lord.

Exit POLONIUS

O, my offence is rank it smells to heaven;
It hath the primal eldest curse upon't,
A brother's murder. Pray can I not,
Though inclination be as sharp as will:
My stronger guilt defeats my strong intent;
And, like a man to double business bound,
I stand in pause where I shall first begin,
And both neglect. What if this cursed hand
Were thicker than itself with brother's blood,
Is there not rain enough in the sweet heavens
To wash it white as snow? Whereto serves mercy
But to confront the visage of offence?
And what's in prayer but this two-fold force,
To be forestalled ere we come to fall,
Or pardon'd being down? Then I'll look up;
My fault is past. But, O, what form of prayer
Can serve my turn? 'Forgive me my foul murder'?
That cannot be; since I am still possess'd
Of those effects for which I did the murder,
My crown, mine own ambition and my queen.
May one be pardon'd and retain the offence?

In the corrupted currents of this world
Offence's gilded hand may shove by justice,
And oft 'tis seen the wicked prize itself
Buys out the law: but 'tis not so above;
There is no shuffling, there the action lies
In his true nature; and we ourselves compell'd,
Even to the teeth and forehead of our faults,
To give in evidence. What then? what rests?
Try what repentance can: what can it not?
Yet what can it when one can not repent?
O wretched state! O bosom black as death!
O limed soul, that, struggling to be free,
Art more engaged! Help, angels! Make assay!
Bow, stubborn knees; and, heart with strings of
    steel,
Be soft as sinews of the newborn babe!
All may be well.
Retires and kneels

Enter HAMLET
HAMLET
Now might I do it pat, now he is praying;
And now I'll do't. And so he goes to heaven;
And so am I revenged. That would be scann'd:
A villain kills my father; and for that,
I, his sole son, do this same villain send
To heaven.

O, this is hire and salary, not revenge.
He took my father grossly, full of bread;
With all his crimes broad blown, as flush as
    May;
And how his audit stands who knows save
    heaven?
But in our circumstance and course of thought,
'Tis heavy with him: and am I then revenged,
To take him in the purging of his soul,
When he is fit and season'd for his passage?
No!
Up, sword; and know thou a more horrid hent:
When he is drunk asleep, or in his rage,
Or in the incestuous pleasure of his bed;
At gaming, swearing, or about some act
That has no relish of salvation in't;
Then trip him, that his heels may kick at heaven,
And that his soul may be as damn'd and black
As hell, whereto it goes. My mother stays:
This physic but prolongs thy sickly days.

Exit

KING CLAUDIUS

    (Rising) My words fly up, my thoughts remain
        below:
    Words without thoughts never to heaven go.

Exit

SCENE IV. THE QUEEN'S CLOSET.

Enter QUEEN GERTRUDE and POLONIUS
LORD POLONIUS

He will come straight. Look you lay home to
him:

Tell him his pranks have been too broad to bear
with,

And that your grace hath screen'd and stood
between

Much heat and him. I'll sconce me even here.

Pray you, be round with him.

HAMLET

(Within) Mother, mother, mother!

QUEEN GERTRUDE

I'll warrant you,

Fear me not: withdraw, I hear him coming.
POLONIUS hides behind the arras

Enter HAMLET
HAMLET

Now, mother, what's the matter?

QUEEN GERTRUDE

Hamlet, thou hast thy father much offended.

HAMLET

Mother, you have my father much offended.

QUEEN GERTRUDE

Come, come, you answer with an idle tongue.

HAMLET

Go, go, you question with a wicked tongue.

QUEEN GERTRUDE

Why, how now, Hamlet!

HAMLET

What's the matter now?

QUEEN GERTRUDE

Have you forgot me?

HAMLET

No, by the rood, not so:

You are the queen, your husband's brother's wife;

And—would it were not so!—you are my
mother.

QUEEN GERTRUDE

Nay, then, I'll set those to you that can speak.

HAMLET

Come, come, and sit you down; you shall not
budge;

You go not till I set you up a glass

Where you may see the inmost part of you.

QUEEN GERTRUDE

What wilt thou do? thou wilt not murder me?

Help, help, ho!

LORD POLONIUS

(Behind) What, ho! help, help, help!

HAMLET

(Drawing) How now! a rat? Dead, for a ducat,
dead!

Makes a pass through the arras

LORD POLONIUS

(Behind) O, I am slain!

Falls and dies

QUEEN GERTRUDE

O me, what hast thou done?

HAMLET

Nay, I know not:
Is it the king?

QUEEN GERTRUDE

O, what a rash and bloody deed is this!

HAMLET

A bloody deed! almost as bad, good mother,
As kill a king, and marry with his brother.

QUEEN GERTRUDE

As kill a king!

HAMLET

Ay, lady, 'twas my word.

Lifts up the array and discovers POLONIUS

Thou wretched, rash, intruding fool, farewell!
I took thee for thy better: take thy fortune;
Thou find'st to be too busy is some danger.
Leave wringing of your hands: peace! sit you
down,

And let me wring your heart; for so I shall,
If it be made of penetrable stuff,
If damned custom have not brass'd it so
That it is proof and bulwark against sense.
QUEEN GERTRUDE
What have I done, that thou darest wag thy
    tongue
In noise so rude against me?
HAMLET
Such an act
That blurs the grace and blush of modesty,
Calls virtue hypocrite, takes off the rose
From the fair forehead of an innocent love
And sets a blister there, makes marriage-vows
As false as dicers' oaths: O, such a deed
As from the body of contraction plucks
The very soul, and sweet religion makes
A rhapsody of words: heaven's face doth glow:
Yea, this solidity and compound mass,
With tristful visage, as against the doom,
Is thought-sick at the act.
QUEEN GERTRUDE
Ay me, what act,
That roars so loud, and thunders in the index?
HAMLET
Look here, upon this picture, and on this,
The counterfeit presentment of two brothers.

See, what a grace was seated on this brow;
Hyperion's curls; the front of Jove himself;
An eye like Mars, to threaten and command;
A station like the herald Mercury
New-lighted on a heaven-kissing hill;
A combination and a form indeed,
Where every god did seem to set his seal,
To give the world assurance of a man:
This was your husband. Look you now, what
    follows:
Here is your husband; like a mildew'd ear,
Blasting his wholesome brother. Have you
    eyes?
Could you on this fair mountain leave to feed,
And batten on this moor? Ha! have you eyes?
You cannot call it love; for at your age
The hey-day in the blood is tame, it's humble,
And waits upon the judgment: and what
    judgment
Would step from this to this? Sense, sure, you
    have,
Else could you not have motion; but sure, that
    sense
Is apoplex'd; for madness would not err,
Nor sense to ecstasy was ne'er so thrall'd
But it reserved some quantity of choice,
To serve in such a difference. What devil was't

That thus hath cozen'd you at hoodman-blind?
Eyes without feeling, feeling without sight,
Ears without hands or eyes, smelling sans all,
Or but a sickly part of one true sense
Could not so mope.
O shame! where is thy blush? Rebellious hell,
If thou canst mutine in a matron's bones,
To flaming youth let virtue be as wax,
And melt in her own fire: proclaim no shame
When the compulsive ardour gives the charge,
Since frost itself as actively doth burn
And reason panders will.

QUEEN GERTRUDE

O Hamlet, speak no more:
Thou turn'st mine eyes into my very soul;
And there I see such black and grained spots
As will not leave their tinct.

HAMLET

Nay, but to live
In the rank sweat of an enseamed bed,
Stew'd in corruption, honeying and making
love
Over the nasty sty.—

QUEEN GERTRUDE

O, speak to me no more;
These words, like daggers, enter in mine ears;
No more, sweet Hamlet!

HAMLET

    A murderer and a villain;

    A slave that is not twentieth part the tithe

    Of your precedent lord; a vice of kings;

    A cutpurse of the empire and the rule,

    That from a shelf the precious diadem stole,

    And put it in his pocket!

QUEEN GERTRUDE

    No more!

HAMLET

    A king of shreds and patches,—

Enter Ghost

    Save me, and hover o'er me with your wings,

    You heavenly guards! What would your gracious figure?

QUEEN GERTRUDE

    Alas, he's mad!

HAMLET

    Do you not come your tardy son to chide,

    That, lapsed in time and passion, lets go by

    The important acting of your dread command?

    O, say!

GHOST

    Do not forget: this visitation

    Is but to whet thy almost blunted purpose.

    But, look, amazement on thy mother sits:

O, step between her and her fighting soul:
Conceit in weakest bodies strongest works:
Speak to her, Hamlet.
HAMLET
How is it with you, lady?
QUEEN GERTRUDE
Alas, how is't with you,
That you do bend your eye on vacancy
And with the incorporal air do hold discourse?
Forth at your eyes your spirits wildly peep;
And, as the sleeping soldiers in the alarm,
Your bedded hair, like life in excrements,
Starts up, and stands on end. O gentle son,
Upon the heat and flame of thy distemper
Sprinkle cool patience. Whereon do you look?
HAMLET
On him, on him! Look you, how pale he glares!
His form and cause conjoin'd, preaching to stones,
Would make them capable. Do not look upon me;
Lest with this piteous action you convert
My stern effects: then what I have to do
Will want true colour; tears perchance for blood.
QUEEN GERTRUDE
To whom do you speak this?

HAMLET

Do you see nothing there?

QUEEN GERTRUDE

Nothing at all; yet all that is I see.

HAMLET

Nor did you nothing hear?

QUEEN GERTRUDE

No, nothing but ourselves.

HAMLET

Why, look you there! look, how it steals away!

My father, in his habit as he lived!

Look, where he goes, even now, out at the

portal!

Exit Ghost

QUEEN GERTRUDE

This the very coinage of your brain:

This bodiless creation ecstasy

Is very cunning in.

HAMLET

Ecstasy!

My pulse, as yours, doth temperately keep time,

And makes as healthful music: it is not madness

That I have utter'd: bring me to the test,

And I the matter will re-word; which madness

Would gambol from. Mother, for love of grace,

Lay not that mattering unction to your soul,

That not your trespass, but my madness speaks:
It will but skin and film the ulcerous place,
Whilst rank corruption, mining all within,
Infects unseen. Confess yourself to heaven;
Repent what's past; avoid what is to come;
And do not spread the compost on the weeds,
To make them ranker. Forgive me this my
    virtue;
For in the fatness of these pursy times
Virtue itself of vice must pardon beg,
Yea, curb and woo for leave to do him good.

QUEEN GERTRUDE

O Hamlet, thou hast cleft my heart in twain.

HAMLET

O, throw away the worser part of it,
And live the purer with the other half.
Good night: but go not to mine uncle's bed;
Assume a virtue, if you have it not.
That monster, custom, who all sense doth eat,
Of habits devil, is angel yet in this,
That to the use of actions fair and good
He likewise gives a frock or livery,
That aptly is put on. Refrain to-night,
And that shall lend a kind of easiness
To the next abstinence: the next more easy;
For use almost can change the stamp of nature,
And either the devil, or throw him out

With wondrous potency. Once more, good
    night:
And when you are desirous to be bless'd,
I'll blessing beg of you. For this same lord,

Pointing to POLONIUS

I do repent: but heaven hath pleased it so,
To punish me with this and this with me,
That I must be their scourge and minister.
I will bestow him, and will answer well
The death I gave him. So, again, good night.
I must be cruel, only to be kind:
Thus bad begins and worse remains behind.
One word more, good lady.

QUEEN GERTRUDE

What shall I do?

HAMLET

Not this, by no means, that I bid you do:
Let the bloat king tempt you again to bed;
Pinch wanton on your cheek; call you his
    mouse;
And let him, for a pair of reechy kisses,
Or paddling in your neck with his damn'd
    fingers,
Make you to ravel all this matter out,
That I essentially am not in madness,

But mad in craft. 'Twere good you let him
    know;
For who, that's but a queen, fair, sober, wise,
Would from a paddock, from a bat, a gib,
Such dear concernings hide? who would do so?
No, in despite of sense and secrecy,
Unpeg the basket on the house's top.
Let the birds fly, and, like the famous ape,
To try conclusions, in the basket creep,
And break your own neck down.

QUEEN GERTRUDE

Be thou assured, if words be made of breath,
And breath of life, I have no life to breathe
What thou hast said to me.

HAMLET

I must to England; you know that?

QUEEN GERTRUDE

Alack,
I had forgot: 'tis so concluded on.

HAMLET

There's letters seal'd: and my two schoolfellows,
Whom I will trust as I will adders fang'd,
They bear the mandate; they must sweep my
    way,
And marshal me to knavery. Let it work;
For 'tis the sport to have the engineer
Hoist with his own petard: and 't shall go hard

But I will delve one yard below their mines,
And blow them at the moon: O, 'tis most sweet,
When in one line two crafts directly meet.
This man shall set me packing:
I'll lug the guts into the neighbour room.
Mother, good night. Indeed this counsellor
Is now most still, most secret and most grave,
Who was in life a foolish prating knave.
Come, sir, to draw toward an end with you.
Good night, mother.

Exeunt severally; HAMLET
dragging in POLONIUS

Act 4

SCENE I. A ROOM IN THE CASTLE.

Enter KING CLAUDIUS, QUEEN GERTRUDE, ROSENCRANTZ, and GUILDENSTERN

KING CLAUDIUS

> There's matter in these sighs, these profound
> > heaves:
>
> You must translate: 'tis fit we understand them.
>
> Where is your son?

QUEEN GERTRUDE

> Bestow this place on us a little while.
>
> > > *Exeunt ROSENCRANTZ and*
> > > > *GUILDENSTERN*

> Ah, my good lord, what have I seen to-night!

KING CLAUDIUS

> What, Gertrude? How does Hamlet?

QUEEN GERTRUDE

    Mad as the sea and wind, when both contend
    Which is the mightier: in his lawless fit,
    Behind the arras hearing something stir,
    Whips out his rapier, cries, 'A rat, a rat!'
    And, in this brainish apprehension, kills
    The unseen good old man.

KING CLAUDIUS

    O heavy deed!
    It had been so with us, had we been there:
    His liberty is full of threats to all;
    To you yourself, to us, to every one.
    Alas, how shall this bloody deed be answer'd?
    It will be laid to us, whose providence
    Should have kept short, restrain'd and out of
        haunt,
    This mad young man: but so much was our
        love,
    We would not understand what was most fit;
    But, like the owner of a foul disease,
    To keep it from divulging, let it feed
    Even on the pith of Life. Where is he gone?

QUEEN GERTRUDE

    To draw apart the body he hath kill'd:
    O'er whom his very madness, like some ore
    Among a mineral of metals base,
    Shows itself pure; he weeps for what is done.

KING CLAUDIUS
> O Gertrude, come away!
> The sun no sooner shall the mountains touch,
> But we will ship him hence: and this vile deed
> We must, with all our majesty and skill,
> Both countenance and excuse. Ho,
> Guildenstern!

Re-enter ROSENCRANTZ and GUILDENSTERN
> Friends both, go join you with some further
> aid:
> Hamlet in madness hath Polonius slain,
> And from his mother's closet hath he dragg'd
> him:
> Go seek him out; speak fair, and bring the body
> Into the chapel. I pray you, haste in this.
>> *Exeunt ROSENCRANTZ and*
>> *GUILDENSTERN*

> Come, Gertrude, we'll call up our wisest friends;
> And let them know, both what we mean to do,
> And what's untimely done. O, come away!
> My soul is full of discord and dismay.
>> *Exeunt*

SCENE II. ANOTHER ROOM IN THE CASTLE.

Enter HAMLET

HAMLET

Safely stowed.

ROSENCRANTZ AND GUILDENSTERN

(Within) Hamlet! Lord Hamlet!

HAMLET

What noise? who calls on Hamlet?

O, here they come.

Enter ROSENCRANTZ and GUILDENSTERN

ROSENCRANTZ

What have you done, my lord, with the dead
body?

HAMLET

Compounded it with dust, whereto 'tis kin.

ROSENCRANTZ

Tell us where 'tis, that we may take it thence
And bear it to the chapel.

HAMLET

Do not believe it.

ROSENCRANTZ

Believe what?

HAMLET

That I can keep your counsel and not mine own.

Besides, to be demanded of a sponge! what replication should be made by the son of a king?

ROSENCRANTZ

Take you me for a sponge, my lord?

HAMLET

Ay, sir, that soaks up the king's countenance, his rewards, his authorities. But such officers do the king best service in the end: he keeps them, like an ape, in the corner of his jaw; first mouthed, to be last swallowed: when he needs what you have gleaned, it is but squeezing you, and, sponge, you shall be dry again.

ROSENCRANTZ

I understand you not, my lord.

HAMLET

I am glad of it: a knavish speech sleeps in a foolish ear.

ROSENCRANTZ

My lord, you must tell us where the body is, and go with us to the king.

HAMLET

The body is with the king, but the king is not with the body. The king is a thing—

GUILDENSTERN

A thing, my lord!

HAMLET

> Of nothing: bring me to him. Hide fox, and all after.

Exeunt

SCENE III. ANOTHER ROOM IN THE CASTLE.

Enter KING CLAUDIUS, attended

KING CLAUDIUS

> I have sent to seek him, and to find the body.
> How dangerous is it that this man goes loose!
> Yet must not we put the strong law on him:
> He's loved of the distracted multitude,
> Who like not in their judgment, but their eyes;
> And where 'tis so, the offender's scourge is
>   weigh'd,
> But never the offence. To bear all smooth
>   and even,
> This sudden sending him away must seem
> Deliberate pause: diseases desperate grown
> By desperate appliance are relieved,
> Or not at all.

Enter ROSENCRANTZ

> How now! what hath befall'n?

ROSENCRANTZ

Where the dead body is bestow'd, my lord,

We cannot get from him.

KING CLAUDIUS

But where is he?

ROSENCRANTZ

Without, my lord; guarded, to know your pleasure.

KING CLAUDIUS

Bring him before us.

ROSENCRANTZ

Ho, Guildenstern! bring in my lord.

Enter HAMLET and GUILDENSTERN

KING CLAUDIUS

Now, Hamlet, where's Polonius?

HAMLET

At supper.

KING CLAUDIUS

At supper! where?

HAMLET

Not where he eats, but where he is eaten: a certain convocation of politic worms are e'en at him. Your worm is your only emperor for diet: we fat all creatures else to fat us, and we fat ourselves for maggots: your fat king and your lean beggar is but variable service, two dishes, but to one table: that's the end.

KING CLAUDIUS

Alas, alas!

HAMLET

A man may fish with the worm that hath eat of a king, and cat of the fish that hath fed of that worm.

KING CLAUDIUS

What dost you mean by this?

HAMLET

Nothing but to show you how a king may go a progress through the guts of a beggar.

KING CLAUDIUS

Where is Polonius?

HAMLET

In heaven; send hither to see: if your messenger find him not there, seek him i' the other place yourself. But indeed, if you find him not within this month, you shall nose him as you go up the stairs into the lobby.

KING CLAUDIUS

Go seek him there.

To some Attendants

HAMLET

He will stay till ye come.

Exeunt Attendants

KING CLAUDIUS

> Hamlet, this deed, for thine especial safety—
> Which we do tender, as we dearly grieve
> For that which thou hast done—must send thee hence
> With fiery quickness: therefore prepare thyself;
> The bark is ready, and the wind at help,
> The associates tend, and every thing is bent
> For England.

HAMLET

> For England!

KING CLAUDIUS

> Ay, Hamlet.

HAMLET

> Good.

KING CLAUDIUS

> So is it, if thou knew'st our purposes.

HAMLET

> I see a cherub that sees them. But, come; for
> England! Farewell, dear mother.

KING CLAUDIUS

> Thy loving father, Hamlet.

HAMLET

> My mother: father and mother is man and wife;
> man and wife is one flesh; and so, my mother.
> Come, for England!

Exit

KING CLAUDIUS

Follow him at foot; tempt him with speed aboard;
Delay it not; I'll have him hence to-night:
Away! for every thing is seal'd and done
That else leans on the affair: pray you, make haste.

Exeunt ROSENCRANTZ and
GUILDENSTERN

And, England, if my love thou hold'st at aught—
As my great power thereof may give thee sense,
Since yet thy cicatrice looks raw and red
After the Danish sword, and thy free awe
Pays homage to us—thou mayst not coldly set
Our sovereign process; which imports at full,
By letters congruing to that effect,
The present death of Hamlet. Do it, England;
For like the hectic in my blood he rages,
And thou must cure me: till I know 'tis done,
Howe'er my haps, my joys were ne'er begun.

Exit

SCENE IV. A PLAIN IN DENMARK.

Enter FORTINBRAS, a Captain, and Soldiers, marching
PRINCE FORTINBRAS

Go, captain, from me greet the Danish king;
Tell him that, by his licence, Fortinbras
Craves the conveyance of a promised march

Over his kingdom. You know the rendezvous.
If that his majesty would aught with us,
We shall express our duty in his eye;
And let him know so.

CAPTAIN

I will do't, my lord.

PRINCE FORTINBRAS

Go softly on.

Exeunt FORTINBRAS and Soldiers

Enter HAMLET, ROSENCRANTZ,
GUILDENSTERN, and others

HAMLET

Good sir, whose powers are these?

CAPTAIN

They are of Norway, sir.

HAMLET

How purposed, sir, I pray you?

CAPTAIN

Against some part of Poland.

HAMLET

Who commands them, sir?

CAPTAIN

The nephews to old Norway, Fortinbras.

HAMLET

Goes it against the main of Poland, sir,
Or for some frontier?

CAPTAIN

Truly to speak, and with no addition,
We go to gain a little patch of ground
That hath in it no profit but the name.
To pay five ducats, five, I would not farm it;
Nor will it yield to Norway or the Pole
A ranker rate, should it be sold in fee.

HAMLET

Why, then the Polack never will defend it.

CAPTAIN

Yes, it is already garrison'd.

HAMLET

Two thousand souls and twenty thousand ducats
Will not debate the question of this straw:
This is the imposthume of much wealth and
    peace,
That inward breaks, and shows no cause without
Why the man dies. I humbly thank you, sir.

CAPTAIN

God be wi' you, sir.

Exit

ROSENCRANTZ

Wilt please you go, my lord?

HAMLET

I'll be with you straight go a little before.

Exeunt all except HAMLET

How all occasions do inform against me,
And spur my dull revenge! What is a man,
If his chief good and market of his time
Be but to sleep and feed? a beast, no more.
Sure, he that made us with such large discourse,
Looking before and after, gave us not
That capability and god-like reason
To fust in us unused. Now, whether it be
Bestial oblivion, or some craven scruple
Of thinking too precisely on the event,
A thought which, quarter'd, hath but one part
    wisdom
And ever three parts coward, I do not know
Why yet I live to say 'This thing's to do;'
Sith I have cause and will and strength and means
To do't. Examples gross as earth exhort me:
Witness this army of such mass and charge
Led by a delicate and tender prince,
Whose spirit with divine ambition puff'd
Makes mouths at the invisible event,
Exposing what is mortal and unsure
To all that fortune, death and danger dare,
Even for an egg-shell. Rightly to be great
Is not to stir without great argument,
But greatly to find quarrel in a straw
When honour's at the stake. How stand I then,
That have a father kill'd, a mother stain'd,

Excitements of my reason and my blood,
And let all sleep? while, to my shame, I see
The imminent death of twenty thousand men,
That, for a fantasy and trick of fame,
Go to their graves like beds, fight for a plot
Whereon the numbers cannot try the cause,
Which is not tomb enough and continent
To hide the slain? O, from this time forth,
My thoughts be bloody, or be nothing worth!

Exit

SCENE V. ELSINORE.
A ROOM IN THE CASTLE.

*Enter QUEEN GERTRUDE, HORATIO, and a
Gentleman*

QUEEN GERTRUDE

    I will not speak with her.

GENTLEMAN

    She is importunate, indeed distract:
    Her mood will needs be pitied.

QUEEN GERTRUDE

    What would she have?

GENTLEMAN

    She speaks much of her father; says she hears
    There's tricks i' the world; and hems, and beats
        her heart;

Spurns enviously at straws; speaks things in
    doubt,
That carry but half sense: her speech is nothing,
Yet the unshaped use of it doth move
The hearers to collection; they aim at it,
And botch the words up fit to their own thoughts;
Which, as her winks, and nods, and gestures
    yield them,
Indeed would make one think there might
    be thought,
Though nothing sure, yet much unhappily.

HORATIO

'Twere good she were spoken with; for she
    may strew
Dangerous conjectures in ill-breeding minds.

QUEEN GERTRUDE

Let her come in.

Exit HORATIO

To my sick soul, as sin's true nature is,
Each toy seems prologue to some great amiss:
So full of artless jealousy is guilt,
It spills itself in fearing to be spilt.

Re-enter HORATIO, with OPHELIA

OPHELIA

Where is the beauteous majesty of Denmark?

QUEEN GERTRUDE

How now, Ophelia!

OPHELIA

(Sings)

How should I your true love know

From another one?

By his cockle hat and staff,

And his sandal shoon.

QUEEN GERTRUDE

Alas, sweet lady, what imports this song?

OPHELIA

Say you? nay, pray you, mark.

Sings

He is dead and gone, lady,

He is dead and gone;

At his head a grass-green turf,

At his heels a stone.

QUEEN GERTRUDE

Nay, but, Ophelia—

OPHELIA

Pray you, mark.

Sings

White his shroud as the mountain snow—

Enter KING CLAUDIUS

QUEEN GERTRUDE

Alas, look here, my lord.

OPHELIA
(Sings)
Larded with sweet flowers
Which bewept to the grave did go
With true-love showers.
KING CLAUDIUS
How do you, pretty lady?
OPHELIA
Well, God 'ild you! They say the owl was a baker's
daughter. Lord, we know what we are, but know
not what we may be. God be at your table!
KING CLAUDIUS
Conceit upon her father.
OPHELIA
Pray you, let's have no words of this; but when
they ask you what it means, say you this:
Sings
To-morrow is Saint Valentine's day,
All in the morning betime,
And I a maid at your window,
To be your Valentine.
Then up he rose, and donn'd his clothes,
And dupp'd the chamber-door;
Let in the maid, that out a maid
Never departed more.
KING CLAUDIUS
Pretty Ophelia!

OPHELIA

> Indeed, la, without an oath, I'll make an end
> on't:
>
> *Sings*
>
> By Gis and by Saint Charity,
> Alack, and fie for shame!
> Young men will do't, if they come to't;
> By cock, they are to blame.
> Quoth she, before you tumbled me,
> You promised me to wed.
> So would I ha' done, by yonder sun,
> An thou hadst not come to my bed.

KING CLAUDIUS

> How long hath she been thus?

OPHELIA

> I hope all will be well. We must be patient: but
> I cannot choose but weep, to think they should
> lay him i' the cold ground. My brother shall
> know of it: and so I thank you for your good
> counsel. Come, my coach! Good night, ladies;
> good night, sweet ladies; good night, good night.
>
> *Exit*

KING CLAUDIUS

> Follow her close; give her good watch,
> I pray you.
>
> *Exit HORATIO*

O, this is the poison of deep grief; it springs
All from her father's death. O Gertrude,
    Gertrude,
When sorrows come, they come not single spies
But in battalions. First, her father slain:
Next, your son gone; and he most violent
    author
Of his own just remove: the people muddied,
Thick and unwholesome in their thoughts and
    whispers,
For good Polonius' death;
and we have done but greenly,
In hugger-mugger to inter him: poor Ophelia
Divided from herself and her fair judgment,
Without the which we are pictures, or mere
    beasts:
Last, and as much containing as all these,
Her brother is in secret come from France;
Feeds on his wonder, keeps himself in clouds,
And wants not buzzers to infect his ear
With pestilent speeches of his father's death;
Wherein necessity, of matter beggar'd,
Will nothing stick our person to arraign
In ear and ear. O my dear Gertrude, this,
Like to a murdering-piece, in many places
Gives me superfluous death.
A noise within

QUEEN GERTRUDE

Alack, what noise is this?

KING CLAUDIUS

Where are my Switzers? Let them guard the
door.

Enter another Gentleman

What is the matter?

GENTLEMAN

Save yourself, my lord:

The ocean, overpeering of his list,

Eats not the flats with more impetuous haste

Than young Laertes, in a riotous head,

O'erbears your officers. The rabble call him lord;

And, as the world were now but to begin,

Antiquity forgot, custom not known,

The ratifiers and props of every word,

They cry 'Choose we: Laertes shall be king:'

Caps, hands, and tongues, applaud it to the
clouds:

'Laertes shall be king, Laertes king!'

QUEEN GERTRUDE

How cheerfully on the false trail they cry!

O, this is counter, you false Danish dogs!

KING CLAUDIUS

The doors are broke.

Noise within

Enter LAERTES, armed; Danes following

LAERTES

Where is this king? Sirs, stand you all without.

DANES

No, let's come in.

LAERTES

I pray you, give me leave.

DANES

We will, we will.

They retire without the door

LAERTES

I thank you: keep the door. O thou vile king,

Give me my father!

QUEEN GERTRUDE

Calmly, good Laertes.

LAERTES

That drop of blood that's calm proclaims me
    bastard,

Cries cuckold to my father, brands the harlot

Even here, between the chaste unsmirched
    brow

Of my true mother.

KING CLAUDIUS

What is the cause, Laertes,

That thy rebellion looks so giant-like?

Let him go, Gertrude; do not fear our person:

There's such divinity doth hedge a king,

That treason can but peep to what it would,
Acts little of his will. Tell me, Laertes,
Why thou art thus incensed. Let him go,
    Gertrude.
Speak, man.
LAERTES
Where is my father?
KING CLAUDIUS
Dead.
QUEEN GERTRUDE
But not by him.
KING CLAUDIUS
Let him demand his fill.
LAERTES
How came he dead? I'll not be juggled with:
To hell, allegiance! vows, to the blackest devil!
Conscience and grace, to the profoundest pit!
I dare damnation. To this point I stand,
That both the worlds I give to negligence,
Let come what comes; only I'll be revenged
Most thoroughly for my father.
KING CLAUDIUS
Who shall stay you?
LAERTES
My will, not all the world:
And for my means, I'll husband them so well,
They shall go far with little.

KING CLAUDIUS

> Good Laertes,
> If you desire to know the certainty
> Of your dear father's death, is't writ in your
> revenge,
> That, swoopstake, you will draw both friend
> and foe,
> Winner and loser?

LAERTES

> None but his enemies.

KING CLAUDIUS

> Will you know them then?

LAERTES

> To his good friends thus wide I'll ope my arms;
> And like the kind life-rendering pelican,
> Repast them with my blood.

KING CLAUDIUS

> Why, now you speak
> Like a good child and a true gentleman.
> That I am guiltless of your father's death,
> And am most sensible in grief for it,
> It shall as level to your judgment pierce
> As day does to your eye.

DANES

> (Within) Let her come in.

LAERTES

> How now! what noise is that?

    O heat, dry up my brains! tears seven times salt,
    Burn out the sense and virtue of mine eye!
    By heaven, thy madness shall be paid by weight,
    Till our scale turn the beam. O rose of May!
    Dear maid, kind sister, sweet Ophelia!
    O heavens! is't possible, a young maid's wits
    Should be as moral as an old man's life?
    Nature is fine in love, and where 'tis fine,
    It sends some precious instance of itself
    After the thing it loves.

OPHELIA

    (Sings)

    They bore him barefaced on the bier;
    Hey non nonny, nonny, hey nonny;
    And in his grave rain'd many a tear:—
    Fare you well, my dove!

LAERTES

    Hadst thou thy wits, and didst persuade revenge,
    It could not move thus.

OPHELIA

    (Sings)

    You must sing a-down a-down,
    An you call him a-down-a.
    O, how the wheel becomes it! It is the false
    steward, that stole his master's daughter.

LAERTES

This nothing's more than matter.

OPHELIA

There's rosemary, that's for remembrance;
pray, love, remember: and there is pansies.
that's for thoughts.

LAERTES

A document in madness, thoughts and
remembrance fitted.

OPHELIA

There's fennel for you, and columbines: there's
rue for you; and here's some for me: we may
call it herb-grace o' Sundays: O you must wear
your rue with a difference. There's a daisy: I
would give you some violets, but they withered
all when my father died: they say he made a
good end—

Sings

For bonny sweet Robin is all my joy.

LAERTES

Thought and affliction, passion, hell itself,
She turns to favour and to prettiness.

OPHELIA

(Sings)
And will he not come again?
And will he not come again?
No, no, he is dead:

Go to thy death-bed:

He never will come again.

His beard was as white as snow,

All flaxen was his poll:

He is gone, he is gone,

And we cast away moan:

God ha' mercy on his soul!

And of all Christian souls, I pray God. God be
     wi' ye.

Exit

LAERTES

Do you see this, O God?

KING CLAUDIUS

Laertes, I must commune with your grief,

Or you deny me right. Go but apart,

Make choice of whom your wisest friends
     you will.

And they shall hear and judge 'twixt you
     and me:

If by direct or by collateral hand

They find us touch'd, we will our kingdom give,

Our crown, our life, and all that we can ours,

To you in satisfaction; but if not,

Be you content to lend your patience to us,

And we shall jointly labour with your soul

To give it due content.

LAERTES

Let this be so;
His means of death, his obscure funeral—
No trophy, sword, nor hatchment o'er his bones,
No noble rite nor formal ostentation—
Cry to be heard, as 'twere from heaven to earth,
That I must call't in question.

KING CLAUDIUS

So you shall;
And where the offence is let the great axe fall.
I pray you, go with me.

Exeunt

SCENE VI. ANOTHER ROOM IN THE CASTLE.

Enter HORATIO and a Servant

HORATIO

What are they that would speak with me?

SERVANT

Sailors, sir: they say they have letters for you.

HORATIO

Let them come in.

Exit Servant

I do not know from what part of the world
I should be greeted, if not from Lord Hamlet.

FIRST SAILOR

God bless you, sir.

HORATIO

Let him bless thee too.

FIRST SAILOR

He shall, sir, an't please him. There's a letter for you, sir; it comes from the ambassador that was bound for England; if your name be Horatio, as I am let to know it is.

HORATIO

(Reads) 'Horatio, when thou shalt have overlooked this, give these fellows some means to the king: they have letters for him. Ere we were two days old at sea, a pirate of very warlike appointment gave us chase. Finding ourselves too slow of sail, we put on a compelled valour, and in the grapple I boarded them: on the instant they got clear of our ship; so I alone became their prisoner. They have dealt with me like thieves of mercy: but they knew what they did; I am to do a good turn for them. Let the king have the letters I have sent; and repair thou to me with as much speed as thou wouldst fly death. I have words to speak in thine ear will make thee dumb; yet are they much too light for the bore of the matter.

These good fellows will bring thee where I am. Rosencrantz and Guildenstern hold their course for England: of them I have much to tell thee. Farewell.

'He that thou knowest thine, HAMLET.' Come, I will make you way for these your letters; And do't the speedier, that you may direct me To him from whom you brought them.

Exeunt

SCENE VII. ANOTHER ROOM IN THE CASTLE.

Enter KING CLAUDIUS and LAERTES

KING CLAUDIUS

>   Now must your conscience my acquaintance
>   seal,
>   And you must put me in your heart for friend,
>   Sith you have heard, and with a knowing ear,
>   That he which hath your noble father slain
>   Pursued my life.

LAERTES

>   It well appears: but tell me
>   Why you proceeded not against these feats,
>   So crimeful and so capital in nature,
>   As by your safety, wisdom, all things else,
>   You mainly were stirr'd up.

KING CLAUDIUS

    O, for two special reasons;
    Which may to you, perhaps, seem much
        unsinew'd,
    But yet to me they are strong. The queen his
        mother
    Lives almost by his looks; and for myself—
    My virtue or my plague, be it either which—
    She's so conjunctive to my life and soul,
    That, as the star moves not but in his sphere,
    I could not but by her. The other motive,
    Why to a public count I might not go,
    Is the great love the general gender bear him;
    Who, dipping all his faults in their affection,
    Would, like the spring that turneth wood to
        stone,
    Convert his gyves to graces; so that my arrows,
    Too slightly timber'd for so loud a wind,
    Would have reverted to my bow again,
    And not where I had aim'd them.

LAERTES

    And so have I a noble father lost;
    A sister driven into desperate terms,
    Whose worth, if praises may go back again,
    Stood challenger on mount of all the age
    For her perfections: but my revenge will come.

KING CLAUDIUS

Break not your sleeps for that: you must not
think

That we are made of stuff so flat and dull

That we can let our beard be shook with danger

And think it pastime. You shortly shall hear
more:

I loved your father, and we love ourself;

And that, I hope, will teach you to imagine—

Enter a Messenger

How now! what news?

MESSENGER

Letters, my lord, from Hamlet:

This to your majesty; this to the queen.

KING CLAUDIUS

From Hamlet! who brought them?

MESSENGER

Sailors, my lord, they say; I saw them not:

They were given me by Claudio; he received
them

Of him that brought them.

KING CLAUDIUS

Laertes, you shall hear them. Leave us.

Exit Messenger

Reads

'High and mighty, You shall know I am set naked on your kingdom. To-morrow shall I beg leave to see your kingly eyes: when I shall, first asking your pardon thereunto, recount the occasion of my sudden and more strange return. 'HAMLET.'

What should this mean? Are all the rest come back?

Or is it some abuse, and no such thing?

LAERTES

Know you the hand?

KING CLAUDIUS

'Tis Hamlets character. 'Naked!

And in a postscript here, he says 'alone.'

Can you advise me?

LAERTES

I'm lost in it, my lord. But let him come;

It warms the very sickness in my heart,

That I shall live and tell him to his teeth,

'Thus didest thou.'

KING CLAUDIUS

If it be so, Laertes—

As how should it be so? how otherwise?—

Will you be ruled by me?

LAERTES

Ay, my lord;

So you will not o'errule me to a peace.

KING CLAUDIUS

To thine own peace. If he be now return'd,

As checking at his voyage, and that he means

No more to undertake it, I will work him

To an exploit, now ripe in my device,

Under the which he shall not choose but fall:

And for his death no wind of blame shall
     breathe,

But even his mother shall uncharge the practise

And call it accident.

LAERTES

My lord, I will be ruled;

The rather, if you could devise it so

That I might be the organ.

KING CLAUDIUS

It falls right.

You have been talk'd of since your travel much,

And that in Hamlet's hearing, for a quality

Wherein, they say, you shine: your sum of parts

Did not together pluck such envy from him

As did that one, and that, in my regard,

Of the unworthiest siege.

LAERTES

What part is that, my lord?

KING CLAUDIUS

A very riband in the cap of youth,
Yet needful too; for youth no less becomes
The light and careless livery that it wears
Than settled age his sables and his weeds,
Importing health and graveness. Two months
since,
Here was a gentleman of Normandy:—
I've seen myself, and served against, the French,
And they can well on horseback: but this gallant
Had witchcraft in't; he grew unto his seat;
And to such wondrous doing brought his horse,
As he had been incorpsed and demi-natured
With the brave beast: so far he topp'd my thought,
That I, in forgery of shapes and tricks,
Come short of what he did.

LAERTES

A Norman was't?

KING CLAUDIUS

A Norman.

LAERTES

Upon my life, Lamond.

KING CLAUDIUS

The very same.

LAERTES

    I know him well: he is the brooch indeed

    And gem of all the nation.

KING CLAUDIUS

    He made confession of you,

    And gave you such a masterly report

    For art and exercise in your defence

    And for your rapier most especially,

    That he cried out, 'twould be a sight indeed,

    If one could match you: the scrimers of their

        nation,

    He swore, had had neither motion, guard, nor

        eye,

    If you opposed them. Sir, this report of his

    Did Hamlet so envenom with his envy

    That he could nothing do but wish and beg

    Your sudden coming o'er, to play with him.

    Now, out of this—

LAERTES

    What out of this, my lord?

KING CLAUDIUS

    Laertes, was your father dear to you?

    Or are you like the painting of a sorrow,

    A face without a heart?

LAERTES

    Why ask you this?

KING CLAUDIUS

Not that I think you did not love your father;
But that I know love is begun by time;
And that I see, in passages of proof,
Time qualifies the spark and fire of it.
There lives within the very flame of love
A kind of wick or snuff that will abate it;
And nothing is at a like goodness still;
For goodness, growing to a plurisy,
Dies in his own too much: that we would do
We should do when we would; for this 'would'
    changes
And hath abatements and delays as many
As there are tongues, are hands, are accidents;
And then this 'should' is like a spendthrift sigh,
That hurts by easing. But, to the quick o' the
    ulcer:—
Hamlet comes back: what would you undertake,
To show yourself your father's son in deed
More than in words?

LAERTES

To cut his throat i' the church.

KING CLAUDIUS

No place, indeed, should murder sanctuarize;
Revenge should have no bounds. But, good
    Laertes,
Will you do this, keep close within your chamber.

Hamlet return'd shall know you are come home:
We'll put on those shall praise your excellence
And set a double varnish on the fame
The Frenchman gave you, bring you in fine
    together
And wager on your heads: he, being remiss,
Most generous and free from all contriving,
Will not peruse the foils; so that, with ease,
Or with a little shuffling, you may choose
A sword unbated, and in a pass of practise
Requite him for your father.

LAERTES

I will do't:
And, for that purpose, I'll anoint my sword.
I bought an unction of a mountebank,
So mortal that, but dip a knife in it,
Where it draws blood no cataplasm so rare,
Collected from all simples that have virtue
Under the moon, can save the thing from death
That is but scratch'd withal: I'll touch my point
With this contagion, that, if I gall him slightly,
It may be death.

KING CLAUDIUS

Let's further think of this;
Weigh what convenience both of time and
    means
May fit us to our shape: if this should fail,

And that our drift look through our bad performance,
'Twere better not assay'd: therefore this project
Should have a back or second, that might hold,
If this should blast in proof. Soft! let me see:
We'll make a solemn wager on your cunnings:
I ha't.
When in your motion you are hot and dry—
As make your bouts more violent to that end—
And that he calls for drink, I'll have prepared him
A chalice for the nonce, whereon but sipping,
If he by chance escape your venom'd stuck,
Our purpose may hold there.

Enter QUEEN GERTRUDE

How now, sweet queen!

QUEEN GERTRUDE

One woe doth tread upon another's heel,
So fast they follow; your sister's drown'd, Laertes.

LAERTES

Drown'd! O, where?

QUEEN GERTRUDE

There is a willow grows aslant a brook,
That shows his hoar leaves in the glassy stream;
There with fantastic garlands did she come

Of crow-flowers, nettles, daisies, and long
    purples
That liberal shepherds give a grosser name,
But our cold maids do dead men's fingers call
    them:
There, on the pendent boughs her coronet
    weeds
Clambering to hang, an envious sliver broke;
When down her weedy trophies and herself
Fell in the weeping brook. Her clothes spread
    wide;
And, mermaid-like, awhile they bore her up:
Which time she chanted snatches of old tunes;
As one incapable of her own distress,
Or like a creature native and indued
Unto that element: but long it could not be
Till that her garments, heavy with their drink,
Pull'd the poor wretch from her melodious lay
To muddy death.

LAERTES

Alas, then, she is drown'd?

QUEEN GERTRUDE

Drown'd, drown'd.

LAERTES

Too much of water hast thou, poor Ophelia,
And therefore I forbid my tears: but yet
It is our trick; nature her custom holds,

Let shame say what it will: when these are gone,
The woman will be out. Adieu, my lord:
I have a speech of fire, that fain would blaze,
But that this folly douts it.

Exit

KING CLAUDIUS
Let's follow, Gertrude:
How much I had to do to calm his rage!
Now fear I this will give it start again;
Therefore let's follow.

Exeunt

Act 5

SCENE I. A CHURCHYARD.

Enter two Clowns, with spades, & c

FIRST CLOWN

Is she to be buried in Christian burial that wilfully seeks her own salvation?

SECOND CLOWN

I tell thee she is: and therefore make her grave straight: the crowner hath sat on her, and finds it Christian burial.

FIRST CLOWN

How can that be, unless she drowned herself in her own defence?

SECOND CLOWN

Why, 'tis found so.

FIRST CLOWN

It must be 'se offendendo;' it cannot be else.

For here lies the point: if I drown myself wittingly, it argues an act: and an act hath three branches: it is, to act, to do, to perform: argal, she drowned herself wittingly.

SECOND CLOWN

Nay, but hear you, goodman delver—

FIRST CLOWN

Give me leave. Here lies the water; good: here stands the man; good; if the man go to this water, and drown himself, it is, will he, nill he, he goes—mark you that; but if the water come to him and drown him, he drowns not himself: argal, he that is not guilty of his own death shortens not his own life.

SECOND CLOWN

But is this law?

FIRST CLOWN

Ay, marry, is't; crowner's quest law.

SECOND CLOWN

Will you ha' the truth on't? If this had not been a gentlewoman, she should have been buried out o' Christian burial.

FIRST CLOWN

Why, there thou say'st: and the more pity that great folk should have countenance in this world to drown or hang themselves, more than their even Christian. Come, my spade. There is no ancient gentleman but gardeners, ditchers, and grave-makers: they hold up Adam's profession.

SECOND CLOWN

Was he a gentleman?

FIRST CLOWN

He was the first that ever bore arms.

SECOND CLOWN

Why, he had none.

FIRST CLOWN

What, art a heathen? How dost thou understand the Scripture? The Scripture says 'Adam digged:' could he dig without arms? I'll put another question to thee: if thou answerest me not to the purpose, confess thyself—

SECOND CLOWN

Go to.

FIRST CLOWN

What is he that builds stronger than either the mason, the shipwright, or the carpenter?

SECOND CLOWN

The gallows-maker; for that frame outlives a thousand tenants.

FIRST CLOWN

I like thy wit well, in good faith: the gallows does well; but how does it well? it does well to those that do in: now thou dost ill to say

the gallows is built stronger than the church:
argal, the gallows may do well to thee. To't
again, come.

SECOND CLOWN

'Who builds stronger than a mason, a
shipwright, or a carpenter?'

FIRST CLOWN

Ay, tell me that, and unyoke.

SECOND CLOWN

Marry, now I can tell.

FIRST CLOWN

To't.

SECOND CLOWN

Mass, I cannot tell.

Enter HAMLET and HORATIO, at a distance

FIRST CLOWN

Cudgel thy brains no more about it, for your
dull ass will not mend his pace with beating;
and, when you are asked this question next, say
'a grave-maker': the houses that he makes last
till doomsday. Go, get thee to Yaughan: fetch
me a stoup of liquor.

Exit Second Clown

He digs and sings
In youth, when I did love, did love,

Methought it was very sweet,

To contract, O, the time, for, ah, my behove,

O, methought, there was nothing meet.

HAMLET

Has this fellow no feeling of his business, that
he sings at grave-making?

HORATIO

Custom hath made it in him a property of
easiness.

HAMLET

'Tis e'en so: the hand of little employment hath
the daintier sense.

FIRST CLOWN

(Sings)

But age, with his stealing steps,

Hath claw'd me in his clutch,

And hath shipped me intil the land,

As if I had never been such.

Throws up a skull

HAMLET

That skull had a tongue in it, and could sing
once: how the knave jowls it to the ground,
as if it were Cain's jaw-bone, that did the first
murder! It might be the pate of a politician,
which this ass now o'er-reaches; one that
would circumvent God, might it not?

HORATIO

It might, my lord.

HAMLET

Or of a courtier; which could say 'Good morrow, sweet lord! How dost thou, good lord?' This might be my lord such-a-one, that praised my lord such-a-one's horse, when he meant to beg it; might it not?

HORATIO

Ay, my lord.

HAMLET

Why, e'en so: and now my Lady Worm's; chapless, and knocked about the mazzard with a sexton's spade: here's fine revolution, an we had the trick to see't. Did these bones cost no more the breeding, but to play at loggats with 'em? mine ache to think on't.

FIRST CLOWN

(Sings)

A pick-axe, and a spade, a spade,
For and a shrouding sheet:
O, a pit of clay for to be made
For such a guest is meet.

Throws up another skull

HAMLET

There's another: why may not that be the skull of a lawyer? Where be his quiddities now, his quillets, his cases, his tenures, and his tricks? why does he suffer this rude knave now to knock him about the sconce with a dirty shovel, and will not tell him of his action of battery? Hum! This fellow might be in's time a great buyer of land, with his statutes, his recognizances, his fines, his double vouchers, his recoveries: is this the fine of his fines, and the recovery of his recoveries, to have his fine pate full of fine dirt? will his vouchers vouch him no more of his purchases, and double ones too, than the length and breadth of a pair of indentures? The very conveyances of his lands will hardly lie in this box; and must the inheritor himself have no more, ha?

HORATIO

Not a jot more, my lord.

HAMLET

Is not parchment made of sheepskins?

HORATIO

Ay, my lord, and of calf-skins too.

HAMLET

They are sheep and calves which seek out assurance in that. I will speak to this fellow. Whose grave's this, sirrah?

FIRST CLOWN

Mine, sir.

O, a pit of clay for to be made

For such a guest is meet.

HAMLET

I think it be thine, indeed; for thou liest in't.

FIRST CLOWN

You lie out on't, sir, and therefore it is not yours: for my part, I do not lie in't, and yet it is mine.

HAMLET

Thou dost lie in't, to be in't and say it is thine: 'tis for the dead, not for the quick; therefore thou liest.

FIRST CLOWN

'Tis a quick lie, sir; 'twill away gain, from me to you.

HAMLET

What man dost thou dig it for?

FIRST CLOWN

For no man, sir.

HAMLET

What woman, then?

FIRST CLOWN

For none, neither.

HAMLET

Who is to be buried in't?

FIRST CLOWN

One that was a woman, sir; but, rest her soul, she's dead.

HAMLET

How absolute the knave is! we must speak by the card, or equivocation will undo us. By the Lord, Horatio, these three years I have taken a note of it; the age is grown so picked that the toe of the peasant comes so near the heel of the courtier, he gaffs his kibe. How long hast thou been a grave-maker?

FIRST CLOWN

Of all the days i' the year, I came to't that day that our last king Hamlet overcame Fortinbras.

HAMLET

How long is that since?

FIRST CLOWN

Cannot you tell that? every fool can tell that: it was the very day that young Hamlet was born; he that is mad, and sent into England.

HAMLET

Ay, marry, why was he sent into England?

FIRST CLOWN

Why, because he was mad: he shall recover his wits there; or, if he do not, it's no great matter there.

HAMLET

Why?

FIRST CLOWN

'Twill, a not be seen in him there; there the men are as mad as he.

HAMLET

How came he mad?

FIRST CLOWN

Very strangely, they say.

HAMLET

How strangely?

FIRST CLOWN

Faith, e'en with losing his wits.

HAMLET

Upon what ground?

FIRST CLOWN

Why, here in Denmark: I have been sexton here, man and boy, thirty years.

HAMLET

How long will a man lie i' the earth ere he rot?

FIRST CLOWN

I' faith, if he be not rotten before he die—as we have many pocky corses now-a-days, that will scarce hold the laying in—he will last you some eight year or nine year: a tanner will last you nine year.

HAMLET

Why he more than another?

FIRST CLOWN

Why, sir, his hide is so tanned with his trade, that he will keep out water a great while; and your water is a sore decayer of your whoreson dead body. Here's a skull now; this skull has lain in the earth three and twenty years.

HAMLET

Whose was it?

FIRST CLOWN

A whoreson mad fellow's it was: whose do you think it was?

HAMLET

Nay, I know not.

FIRST CLOWN

A pestilence on him for a mad rogue! a' poured a flagon of Rhenish on my head once. This same skull, sir, was Yorick's skull, the king's jester.

HAMLET

This?

FIRST CLOWN

E'en that.

HAMLET

Let me see.

Takes the skull

Alas, poor Yorick! I knew him, Horatio: a fellow of infinite jest, of most excellent fancy: he hath borne me on his back a thousand times; and now, how abhorred in my imagination it is! my gorge rims at it. Here hung those lips that I have kissed I know not how oft. Where be your gibes now? your gambols? your songs? your flashes of merriment, that were wont to set the table on a roar? Not one now, to mock your own grinning? quite chap-fallen? Now get you to my lady's chamber, and tell her, let her paint an inch thick, to this favour she must come; make her laugh at that. Prithee, Horatio, tell me one thing.

HORATIO

What's that, my lord?

HAMLET

Dost thou think Alexander looked o' this fashion i' the earth?

HORATIO

E'en so.

HAMLET

And smelt so? pah!

Puts down the skull

HORATIO

E'en so, my lord.

HAMLET

To what base uses we may return, Horatio!
Why may not imagination trace the noble dust
of Alexander, till he find it stopping a bung-
hole?

HORATIO

'Twere to consider too curiously, to consider
so.

HAMLET

No, faith, not a jot; but to follow him thither
with modesty enough, and likelihood to lead it:
as thus: Alexander died, Alexander was buried,
Alexander returneth into dust; the dust is
earth; of earth we make loam; and why of that
loam, whereto he was converted, might they
not stop a beer-barrel? Imperious Caesar, dead
and turn'd to clay, Might stop a hole to keep
the wind away: O, that that earth, which kept
the world in awe, Should patch a wall to expel
the winter flaw! But soft! but soft! aside: here
comes the king.

*Enter Priest, & c. in procession; the Corpse of
OPHELIA, LAERTES and Mourners following;
KING CLAUDIUS, QUEEN GERTRUDE, their
trains, & c*

The queen, the courtiers: who is this they
follow?
And with such maimed rites? This doth betoken
The corse they follow did with desperate hand
Fordo its own life: 'twas of some estate.
Couch we awhile, and mark.

Retiring with HORATIO

LAERTES

What ceremony else?

HAMLET

That is Laertes,
A very noble youth: mark.

LAERTES

What ceremony else?

FIRST PRIEST

Her obsequies have been as far enlarged
As we have warrantise: her death was doubtful;
And, but that great command o'ersways the
    order,
She should in ground unsanctified have lodged
Till the last trumpet: for charitable prayers,
Shards, flints and pebbles should be thrown
    on her;
Yet here she is allow'd her virgin crants,
Her maiden strewments and the bringing home
Of bell and burial.

LAERTES

Must there no more be done?

FIRST PRIEST

No more be done:

We should profane the service of the dead

To sing a requiem and such rest to her

As to peace-parted souls.

LAERTES

Lay her i' the earth:

And from her fair and unpolluted flesh

May violets spring! I tell thee, churlish priest,

A ministering angel shall my sister be,

When thou liest howling.

HAMLET

What, the fair Ophelia!

QUEEN GERTRUDE

Sweets to the sweet: farewell!

Scattering flowers

I hoped thou shouldst have been my Hamlet's
wife;

I thought thy bride-bed to have deck'd, sweet
maid,

And not have strew'd thy grave.

LAERTES

O, treble woe

Fall ten times treble on that cursed head,

Whose wicked deed thy most ingenious sense

Deprived thee of! Hold off the earth awhile,
Till I have caught her once more in mine arms:
Leaps into the grave
Now pile your dust upon the quick and dead,
Till of this flat a mountain you have made,
To o'ertop old Pelion, or the skyish head
Of blue Olympus.

HAMLET

(Advancing) What is he whose grief
Bears such an emphasis? whose phrase of sorrow
Conjures the wandering stars, and makes them stand
Like wonder-wounded hearers? This is I,
Hamlet the Dane.
Leaps into the grave

LAERTES

The devil take thy soul!
Grappling with him

HAMLET

Thou pray'st not well.
I prithee, take thy fingers from my throat;
For, though I am not splenitive and rash,
Yet have I something in me dangerous,
Which let thy wiseness fear: hold off thy hand.

KING CLAUDIUS

Pluck them asunder.

QUEEN GERTRUDE

Hamlet, Hamlet!

ALL

Gentlemen—

HORATIO

Good my lord, be quiet.

The Attendants part them, and they come out of the grave

HAMLET

Why I will fight with him upon this theme

Until my eyelids will no longer wag.

QUEEN GERTRUDE

O my son, what theme?

HAMLET

I loved Ophelia: forty thousand brothers

Could not, with all their quantity of love,

Make up my sum. What wilt thou do for her?

KING CLAUDIUS

O, he is mad, Laertes.

QUEEN GERTRUDE

For love of God, forbear him.

HAMLET

'Swounds, show me what thou'lt do:

Woo't weep? woo't fight? woo't fast? woo't tear

thyself?

Woo't drink up eisel? eat a crocodile?

I'll do't. Dost thou come here to whine?

To outface me with leaping in her grave?
Be buried quick with her, and so will I:
And, if thou prate of mountains, let them throw
Millions of acres on us, till our ground,
Singeing his pate against the burning zone,
Make Ossa like a wart! Nay, an thou'lt mouth,
I'll rant as well as thou.

QUEEN GERTRUDE

This is mere madness:
And thus awhile the fit will work on him;
Anon, as patient as the female dove,
When that her golden couplets are disclosed,
His silence will sit drooping.

HAMLET

Hear you, sir;
What is the reason that you use me thus?
I loved you ever: but it is no matter;
Let Hercules himself do what he may,
The cat will mew and dog will have his day.

Exit

KING CLAUDIUS

I pray you, good Horatio, wait upon him.

Exit HORATIO

To LAERTES
Strengthen your patience in our last night's
    speech;
We'll put the matter to the present push.
Good Gertrude, set some watch over your son.
This grave shall have a living monument:
An hour of quiet shortly shall we see;
Till then, in patience our proceeding be.

                        Exeunt

SCENE II. A HALL IN THE CASTLE.

Enter HAMLET and HORATIO

HAMLET
    So much for this, sir: now shall you see the
        other;
    You do remember all the circumstance?

HORATIO
    Remember it, my lord?

HAMLET
    Sir, in my heart there was a kind of fighting,
    That would not let me sleep: methought I lay
    Worse than the mutines in the bilboes. Rashly,
    And praised be rashness for it, let us know,
    Our indiscretion sometimes serves us well,
    When our deep plots do pall: and that should
        teach us

There's a divinity that shapes our ends,
Rough-hew them how we will—
HORATIO
That is most certain.
HAMLET
Up from my cabin,
My sea-gown scarf'd about me, in the dark
Groped I to find out them; had my desire.
Finger'd their packet, and in fine withdrew
To mine own room again; making so bold,
My fears forgetting manners, to unseal
Their grand commission; where I found,
    Horatio—
O royal knavery!—an exact command,
Larded with many several sorts of reasons
Importing Denmark's health and England's too,
With, ho! such bugs and goblins in my life,
That, on the supervise, no leisure bated,
No, not to stay the grinding of the axe,
My head should be struck off.
HORATIO
Is't possible?
HAMLET
Here's the commission: read it at more leisure.
But wilt thou hear me how I did proceed?
HORATIO
I beseech you.

HAMLET

    Being thus be-netted round with villanies—
    Ere I could make a prologue to my brains,
    They had begun the play—I sat me down,
    Devised a new commission, wrote it fair:
    I once did hold it, as our statists do,
    A baseness to write fair and labour'd much
    How to forget that learning, but, sir, now
    It did me yeoman's service: wilt thou know
    The effect of what I wrote?

HORATIO

    Ay, good my lord.

HAMLET

    An earnest conjuration from the king,
    As England was his faithful tributary,
    As love between them like the palm might
        flourish,
    As peace should stiff her wheaten garland wear
    And stand a comma 'tween their amities,
    And many such-like 'As'es of great charge,
    That, on the view and knowing of these
        contents,
    Without debatement further, more or less,
    He should the bearers put to sudden death,
    Not shriving-time allow'd.

HORATIO

    How was this seal'd?

HAMLET

Why, even in that was heaven ordinant.
I had my father's signet in my purse,
Which was the model of that Danish seal;
Folded the writ up in form of the other,
Subscribed it, gave't the impression, placed it
    safely,
The changeling never known. Now, the next
    day
Was our sea-fight; and what to this was sequent
Thou know'st already.

HORATIO

So Guildenstern and Rosencrantz go to't.

HAMLET

Why, man, they did make love to this
    employment;
They are not near my conscience; their defeat
Does by their own insinuation grow:
'Tis dangerous when the baser nature comes
Between the pass and fell incensed points
Of mighty opposites.

HORATIO

Why, what a king is this!

HAMLET

Does it not, think'st thee, stand me now upon—
He that hath kill'd my king and whored my
    mother,

Popp'd in between the election and my hopes,
Thrown out his angle for my proper life,
And with such cozenage—is't not perfect
    conscience,
To quit him with this arm? and is't not to be
    damn'd,
To let this canker of our nature come
In further evil?

HORATIO

It must be shortly known to him from England
What is the issue of the business there.

HAMLET

It will be short: the interim is mine;
And a man's life's no more than to say 'One.'
But I am very sorry, good Horatio,
That to Laertes I forgot myself;
For, by the image of my cause, I see
The portraiture of his: I'll court his favours.
But, sure, the bravery of his grief did put me
Into a towering passion.

HORATIO

Peace! who comes here?

Enter OSRIC

OSRIC

Your lordship is right welcome back to
Denmark.

HAMLET

I humbly thank you, sir. Dost know this water-
fly?

HORATIO

No, my good lord.

HAMLET

Thy state is the more gracious; for 'tis a vice to
know him. He hath much land, and fertile: let a
beast be lord of beasts, and his crib shall stand
at the king's mess: 'tis a chough; but, as I say,
spacious in the possession of dirt.

OSRIC

Sweet lord, if your lordship were at leisure, I
should impart a thing to you from his majesty.

HAMLET

I will receive it, sir, with all diligence of spirit.
Put your bonnet to his right use; 'tis for the head.

OSRIC

I thank your lordship, it is very hot.

HAMLET

No, believe me, 'tis very cold; the wind is
northerly.

OSRIC

It is indifferent cold, my lord, indeed.

HAMLET

But yet methinks it is very sultry and hot for
my complexion.

OSRIC

Exceedingly, my lord; it is very sultry—as 'twere—I cannot tell how. But, my lord, his majesty bade me signify to you that he has laid a great wager on your head: sir, this is the matter—

HAMLET

I beseech you, remember—

HAMLET moves him to put on his hat

OSRIC

Nay, good my lord; for mine ease, in good faith. Sir, here is newly come to court Laertes; believe me, an absolute gentleman, full of most excellent differences, of very soft society and great showing: indeed, to speak feelingly of him, he is the card or calendar of gentry, for you shall find in him the continent of what part a gentleman would see.

HAMLET

Sir, his definement suffers no perdition in you; though, I know, to divide him inventorially would dizzy the arithmetic of memory, and yet but yaw neither, in respect of his quick sail. But, in the verity of extolment, I take him to be a soul of great article; and his infusion of such

dearth and rareness, as, to make true diction of
him, his semblable is his mirror; and who else
would trace him, his umbrage, nothing more.

OSRIC

Your lordship speaks most infallibly of him.

HAMLET

The concernancy, sir? why do we wrap the
gentleman in our more rawer breath?

OSRIC

Sir?

HORATIO

Is't not possible to understand in another
tongue?
You will do't, sir, really.

HAMLET

What imports the nomination of this
gentleman?

OSRIC

Of Laertes?

HORATIO

His purse is empty already; all's golden words
are spent.

HAMLET

Of him, sir.

OSRIC

I know you are not ignorant—

HAMLET

I would you did, sir; yet, in faith, if you did, it would not much approve me. Well, sir?

OSRIC

You are not ignorant of what excellence Laertes is—

HAMLET

I dare not confess that, lest I should compare with him in excellence; but, to know a man well, were to know himself.

OSRIC

I mean, sir, for his weapon; but in the imputation laid on him by them, in his meed he's unfellowed.

HAMLET

What's his weapon?

OSRIC

Rapier and dagger.

HAMLET

That's two of his weapons: but, well.

OSRIC

The king, sir, hath wagered with him six Barbary horses: against the which he has imponed, as I take it, six French rapiers and poniards, with their assigns, as girdle, hangers, and so: three of the carriages, in faith, are very

dear to fancy, very responsive to the hilts, most
delicate carriages, and of very liberal conceit.

HAMLET

What call you the carriages?

HORATIO

I knew you must be edified by the margent ere
you had done.

OSRIC

The carriages, sir, are the hangers.

HAMLET

The phrase would be more german to the
matter, if we could carry cannon by our sides: I
would it might be hangers till then. But, on: six
Barbary horses against six French swords, their
assigns, and three liberal-conceited carriages;
that's the French bet against the Danish. Why
is this 'imponed,' as you call it?

OSRIC

The king, sir, hath laid, that in a dozen passes
between yourself and him, he shall not exceed
you three hits: he hath laid on twelve for nine;
and it would come to immediate trial, if your
lordship would vouchsafe the answer.

HAMLET

How if I answer 'no'?

OSRIC

I mean, my lord, the opposition of your person in trial.

HAMLET

Sir, I will walk here in the hall: if it please his majesty, 'tis the breathing time of day with me; let the foils be brought, the gentleman willing, and the king hold his purpose, I will win for him an I can; if not, I will gain nothing but my shame and the odd hits.

OSRIC

Shall I re-deliver you e'en so?

HAMLET

To this effect, sir; after what flourish your nature will.

OSRIC

I commend my duty to your lordship.

HAMLET

Yours, yours.

Exit OSRIC

He does well to commend it himself; there are no tongues else for's turn.

HORATIO

This lapwing runs away with the shell on his head.

HAMLET

He did comply with his dug, before he sucked it. Thus has he—and many more of the same bevy that I know the dressy age dotes on—only got the tune of the time and outward habit of encounter; a kind of yesty collection, which carries them through and through the most fond and winnowed opinions; and do but blow them to their trial, the bubbles are out.

Enter a Lord

LORD

My lord, his majesty commended him to you by young Osric, who brings back to him that you attend him in the hall: he sends to know if your pleasure hold to play with Laertes, or that you will take longer time.

HAMLET

I am constant to my purpose; they follow the king's pleasure: if his fitness speaks, mine is ready; now or whensoever, provided I be so able as now.

LORD

The king and queen and all are coming down.

HAMLET

In happy time.

LORD

The queen desires you to use some gentle
entertainment to Laertes before you fall to
play.

HAMLET

She well instructs me.

Exit Lord

HORATIO

You will lose this wager, my lord.

HAMLET

I do not think so: since he went into France, I
have been in continual practise: I shall win at
the odds. But thou wouldst not think how ill
all's here about my heart: but it is no matter.

HORATIO

Nay, good my lord—

HAMLET

It is but foolery; but it is such a kind of gain-
giving, as would perhaps trouble a woman.

HORATIO

If your mind dislike any thing, obey it: I will
forestall their repair hither, and say you are
not fit.

HAMLET

Not a whit, we defy augury: there's a special
providence in the fall of a sparrow. If it be now,

'tis not to come; if it be not to come, it will
be now; if it be not now, yet it will come: the
readiness is all: since no man has aught of what
he leaves, what is't to leave betimes?

*Enter KING CLAUDIUS, QUEEN GERTRUDE,
LAERTES, Lords, OSRIC, and Attendants with foils,
&c*

KING CLAUDIUS

Come, Hamlet, come, and take this hand from
me.

*KING CLAUDIUS puts LAERTES' hand into
HAMLET's*

HAMLET

Give me your pardon, sir: I've done you wrong;
But pardon't, as you are a gentleman.
This presence knows,
And you must needs have heard, how I am
    punish'd
With sore distraction. What I have done,
That might your nature, honour and exception
Roughly awake, I here proclaim was madness.
Was't Hamlet wrong'd Laertes? Never Hamlet:
If Hamlet from himself be ta'en away,
And when he's not himself does wrong Laertes,

Then Hamlet does it not, Hamlet denies it.
Who does it, then? His madness: if't be so,
Hamlet is of the faction that is wrong'd;
His madness is poor Hamlet's enemy.
Sir, in this audience,
Let my disclaiming from a purposed evil
Free me so far in your most generous thoughts,
That I have shot mine arrow o'er the house,
And hurt my brother.

LAERTES

I am satisfied in nature,
Whose motive, in this case, should stir me most
To my revenge: but in my terms of honour
I stand aloof; and will no reconcilement,
Till by some elder masters, of known honour,
I have a voice and precedent of peace,
To keep my name ungored. But till that time,
I do receive your offer'd love like love,
And will not wrong it.

HAMLET

I embrace it freely;
And will this brother's wager frankly play.
Give us the foils. Come on.

LAERTES

Come, one for me.

HAMLET

I'll be your foil, Laertes: in mine ignorance

Your skill shall, like a star i' the darkest night,
Stick fiery off indeed.

LAERTES

You mock me, sir.

HAMLET

No, by this hand.

KING CLAUDIUS

Give them the foils, young Osric. Cousin Hamlet,
You know the wager?

HAMLET

Very well, my lord
Your grace hath laid the odds o' the weaker
side.

KING CLAUDIUS

I do not fear it; I have seen you both:
But since he is better'd, we have therefore odds.

LAERTES

This is too heavy, let me see another.

HAMLET

This likes me well. These foils have all a length?
They prepare to play

OSRIC

Ay, my good lord.

KING CLAUDIUS

Set me the stoops of wine upon that table.
If Hamlet give the first or second hit,
Or quit in answer of the third exchange,

Let all the battlements their ordnance fire:
The king shall drink to Hamlet's better breath;
And in the cup an union shall he throw,
Richer than that which four successive kings
In Denmark's crown have worn. Give me the
   cups;
And let the kettle to the trumpet speak,
The trumpet to the cannoneer without,
The cannons to the heavens, the heavens to
   earth,
'Now the king dunks to Hamlet.' Come, begin:
And you, the judges, bear a wary eye.

HAMLET
Come on, sir.

LAERTES
Come, my lord.
They play

HAMLET
One.

LAERTES
No.

HAMLET
Judgment.

OSRIC
A hit, a very palpable hit.

LAERTES
Well; again.

KING CLAUDIUS

Stay; give me drink. Hamlet, this pearl is thine;
Here's to thy health.
Trumpets sound, and cannon shot off within
Give him the cup.

HAMLET

I'll play this bout first; set it by awhile. Come.
They play
Another hit; what say you?

LAERTES

A touch, a touch, I do confess.

KING CLAUDIUS

Our son shall win.

QUEEN GERTRUDE

He's fat, and scant of breath.
Here, Hamlet, take my napkin, rub thy brows;
The queen carouses to thy fortune, Hamlet.

HAMLET

Good madam!

KING CLAUDIUS

Gertrude, do not drink.

QUEEN GERTRUDE

I will, my lord; I pray you, pardon me.

KING CLAUDIUS

(Aside) It is the poison'd cup: it is too late.

HAMLET

I dare not drink yet, madam; by and by.

QUEEN GERTRUDE

Come, let me wipe thy face.

LAERTES

My lord, I'll hit him now.

KING CLAUDIUS

I do not think't.

LAERTES

(Aside) And yet 'tis almost 'gainst my conscience.

HAMLET

Come, for the third, Laertes: you but dally;

I pray you, pass with your best violence;

I am afeard you make a wanton of me.

LAERTES

Say you so? come on.

They play

OSRIC

Nothing, neither way.

LAERTES

Have at you now!

LAERTES wounds HAMLET; then in scuffling, they change rapiers, and HAMLET wounds LAERTES

KING CLAUDIUS

Part them; they are incensed.

HAMLET

Nay, come, again.

OSRIC

Look to the queen there, ho!

HORATIO

They bleed on both sides. How is it, my lord?

OSRIC

How is't, Laertes?

LAERTES

Why, as a woodcock to mine own springe,
     Osric;

I am justly kill'd with mine own treachery.

HAMLET

How does the queen?

KING CLAUDIUS

She swounds to see them bleed.

QUEEN GERTRUDE

No, no, the drink, the drink—O my dear
     Hamlet—

The drink, the drink! I am poison'd.

Dies

HAMLET

O villany! Ho! let the door be lock'd:

Treachery! Seek it out.

LAERTES

It is here, Hamlet: Hamlet, thou art slain;

No medicine in the world can do thee good;

In thee there is not half an hour of life;
The treacherous instrument is in thy hand,
Unbated and envenom'd: the foul practise
Hath turn'd itself on me lo, here I lie,
Never to rise again: thy mother's poison'd:
I can no more: the king, the king's to blame.

HAMLET

The point!—envenom'd too!
Then, venom, to thy work.

Stabs KING CLAUDIUS

ALL

Treason! treason!

KING CLAUDIUS

O, yet defend me, friends; I am but hurt.

HAMLET

Here, thou incestuous, murderous, damned
Dane,
Drink off this potion. Is thy union here?
Follow my mother.

KING CLAUDIUS dies

LAERTES

He is justly served;
It is a poison temper'd by himself.

Exchange forgiveness with me, noble Hamlet:
Mine and my father's death come not upon
    thee,
Nor thine on me.
Dies

HAMLET

Heaven make thee free of it! I follow thee.
I am dead, Horatio. Wretched queen, adieu!
You that look pale and tremble at this chance,
That are but mutes or audience to this act,
Had I but time—as this fell sergeant, death,
Is strict in his arrest—O, I could tell you—
But let it be. Horatio, I am dead;
Thou livest; report me and my cause aright
To the unsatisfied.

HORATIO

Never believe it:
I am more an antique Roman than a Dane:
Here's yet some liquor left.

HAMLET

As thou'rt a man,
Give me the cup: let go; by heaven, I'll have't.
O good Horatio, what a wounded name,
Things standing thus unknown, shall live
    behind me!
If thou didst ever hold me in thy heart
Absent thee from felicity awhile,

And in this harsh world draw thy breath in pain,
To tell my story.
March afar off, and shot within
What warlike noise is this?

OSRIC

Young Fortinbras, with conquest come from
   Poland,
To the ambassadors of England gives
This warlike volley.

HAMLET

O, I die, Horatio;
The potent poison quite o'er-crows my spirit:
I cannot live to hear the news from England;
But I do prophesy the election lights
On Fortinbras: he has my dying voice;
So tell him, with the occurrents, more and less,
Which have solicited. The rest is silence.
Dies

HORATIO

Now cracks a noble heart. Good night sweet
   prince:
And flights of angels sing thee to thy rest!
Why does the drum come hither?
March within

*Enter FORTINBRAS, the English Ambassadors, and
others*

PRINCE FORTINBRAS

Where is this sight?

HORATIO

What is it ye would see?

If aught of woe or wonder, cease your search.

PRINCE FORTINBRAS

This quarry cries on havoc. O proud death,

What feast is toward in thine eternal cell,

That thou so many princes at a shot

So bloodily hast struck?

FIRST AMBASSADOR

The sight is dismal;

And our affairs from England come too late:

The ears are senseless that should give us
     hearing,

To tell him his commandment is fulfill'd,

That Rosencrantz and Guildenstern are dead:

Where should we have our thanks?

HORATIO

Not from his mouth,

Had it the ability of life to thank you:

He never gave commandment for their death.

But since, so jump upon this bloody question,

You from the Polack wars, and you from England,

Are here arrived give order that these bodies

High on a stage be placed to the view;

And let me speak to the yet unknowing world

How these things came about: so shall you hear
Of carnal, bloody, and unnatural acts,
Of accidental judgments, casual slaughters,
Of deaths put on by cunning and forced cause,
And, in this upshot, purposes mistook
Fall'n on the inventors' reads: all this can I
Truly deliver.

PRINCE FORTINBRAS
Let us haste to hear it,
And call the noblest to the audience.
For me, with sorrow I embrace my fortune:
I have some rights of memory in this kingdom,
Which now to claim my vantage doth invite me.

HORATIO
Of that I shall have also cause to speak,
And from his mouth whose voice will draw
    on more;
But let this same be presently perform'd,
Even while men's minds are wild; lest more
    mischance
On plots and errors, happen.

PRINCE FORTINBRAS
Let four captains
Bear Hamlet, like a soldier, to the stage;
For he was likely, had he been put on,
To have proved most royally: and, for his
    passage,

The soldiers' music and the rites of war
Speak loudly for him.
Take up the bodies: such a sight as this
Becomes the field, but here shows much amiss.
Go, bid the soldiers shoot.
A dead march. Exeunt, bearing off the dead bodies;
after which a peal of ordnance is shot off